MY BURNING BUSH

My Spiritual Journey from Judaism to the Lord Jesus Christ

An Autobiography

Written by
Nancy Goldberg Hilton

Edited by
Lynn M. Hilton, PhD

My Burning Bush
Copyright 2006 by Nancy Goldberg Hilton
All rights reserved

Distributed by:

Granite Publishing and Distribution, LLC
868 North 1430 West
Orem, Utah 84057
(801) 229-9023 • Toll Free (800) 574-5779
Fax (801) 229-1924

Cover Design: Steve Gray
Page Layout and Design: Lyndell Lutes

ISBN-13: 978-1-56684-640-0
ISBN-10: 1-56684-640-4
Library of Congress Control Number: 2006926030
First Printing May 2006
10 9 8 7 6 5 4 3 2 1
Printed in the United States of America

Table of Contents

PREFACE—vii

1 • BIRTH AND CAREER (1946–1990) —1
Jewish Heritage 1
My Childhood 2
School and University 4
Career and Marriage 5

2 • MY BURNING BUSH EXPERIENCE (1991–1995)—9
Searching for Answers 9
My Spiritual Battle 1992 11
My Burning Bush —My Miracle at Rainbow Bridge 1992 13
My Search for the Truth about Jesus Christ 18
Visiting Christian Churches 20

3 • MET THE LATTER-DAY SAINTS (1995–1996)—25
The Book of Mormon 25
Learning the First Principles of the Gospel 30
Learning to Pray 32
God 33
Jesus Christ 34
The Holy Ghost 36
The Prophet Joseph Smith and the Restoration of
        The Church of Jesus Christ 37
Restoration of the Priesthood or Authority to Act for God 39
Aaronic Priesthood 40
Melchizedek Priesthood 41
Joseph Smith Translation of the Bible 43
Priesthood Blessings 44

Temples Ancient and Modern 45
Keeping the Commandments 47
Attending Church 49
Procrastinating 51

4 • A MEMBER OF THE CHURCH OF JESUS CHRIST OF
    LATTER-DAY SAINTS (1996)—53
My Faith Is Growing 54
God Revealed the Truth to Me 56
My Baptism 57
God and Jesus Christ Became More Personal to Me 58
The Gift of the Holy Ghost 59
My First Church Calling 59
Lost Books of the Bible 61
Lost Scriptures Restored 63
God Lives and Continues to Communicate 65
Prophets and Apostles 66
Patriarchal Blessing 67
Gospel also Preached in the Spirit World 67
Entering the Temple 69
Purpose of Bloody Sacrifices in the Old Testament 70
Time to Reflect 73

5 • MY FIRST MISSION, TO THE FAMILY HISTORY LIBRARY
    IN SALT LAKE CITY, UTAH (1998–2001)—77
Blessings for My Business 77
Decision to Sell All and Move to Salt Lake City, Utah 78
Jewish Database and Two and One-half Year Mission 80
The IAJGS Award 2001 83

6 • MARRIAGE TO LYNN M. HILTON (2001)—87
Searching for My Husband 87
Introduced by Jess and Patti Shumway 88
Marriage Proposal 91

Telling My Parents 91

Meeting Lynn's Children and Grandchildren 92

Temple Marriage and Sealing in the Salt Lake Temple 93

Foreign Travel 95

The Hilton Family Reunion 96

7 • MISSION WITH ELDER LYNN M. HILTON TO SYDNEY, AUSTRALIA (2002–2003)—97

The Letter from Our Prophet Included Our Mission Call 97

My Father's Death 97

Arrival in Sydney Australia 99

Creating an Employment Program 100

Speaking in Sacrament, Relief Society, and Priesthood Meetings about Employment 100

Youth Career Workshop 102

Better Employment in Building Up the Kingdom of God 102

Working in the Sydney Temple 104

Family History Work in Sydney 104

The End of Our Australian Mission 104

8 • SECOND MISSION WITH ELDER HILTON, EMPLOYMENT SECTION OF THE CHURCH WELFARE DEPARTMENT (2003–2004)—107

Working Together with the Employment Team 107

Wrote the Suggested LDS Employment Program for Wards and Stakes 108

9 • THIRD MISSION WITH ELDER HILTON, GREECE ATHENS MISSION, PART ONE, IRBID JORDAN (2004–2005)—111

Mission Call to Greece Athens Mission in Irbid, Jordan 111

Overcoming Personal Feelings of Fear 112

Preaching the Gospel 115

Humanitarian Work 116

Loving the People, the Lord, and Each Other 117

Family History for Our Jordanian Members and Miracles of
the Spirit from the Other Side of the Veil 117

Bible Sites in Jordan 118

A Special Yearning for Jerusalem 119

10 • GREECE ATHENS MISSION, PART TWO,
ASSIGNMENT IN ATHENS (2005)—121

Directors of the Family History Center in Athens, Greece 121

The Continuing Miracles of Family History Work 123

Baptisms 124

The End of Our Third Mission 124

Our Trip to Israel 125

11 • GROWING SPIRITUALLY —127

What I Learned Since Rainbow Bridge 127

Fulfillment of Promises for the Jewish People 128

My Testimony 130

EXPLANATION OF SOURCES AND REFERENCES

- Books in the Bible are sited with the usual abbreviations.
- JST means Joseph Smith Translation of the Bible found in the footnotes and the Appendix of the Holy Bible, Latter-day Saint edition.
- References to the Book of Mormon use the usual abbreviations.
- Moses means the book of Moses in the Pearl of Great Price and Abraham means book of Abraham in the Pearl of Great Price.

The Book of Mormon, Doctrine and Covenants (D&C), and Pearl of Great Price are the standard works of The Church of Jesus Christ of Latter-day Saints. They can be viewed or purchased at the web site: www.lds.org.

Preface

As I walked under the bridge, I heard one loud clap of thunder! It shook the earth.

The sound coursed through me, and I felt a great change enter my whole being. My mind was instantly opened to understand the things of God. I immediately accepted the reality of God's being. I knew that His Son was Jesus Christ, a person whose love extended out to me at this time of personal crisis. He was truly my Savior at that moment, as all thoughts of my past trials faded and my heart was filled with wonder, compassion, peace, and love. This experience was brief, but its effect on my life will last forever.

I am Jewish and experienced a miracle of God at Rainbow Bridge, Utah in 1992. I felt like Moses standing in front of the burning bush. I was changed in a moment from disbelieving in God to a woman who knew the reality of God and His Son, Jesus Christ.

I have waited thirteen years to write about these personal experiences with God. I feel that the time has come for me to share with you what happened to me. After this miracle I went on a spiritual quest to find out more about Jesus Christ. This is the story of the miracle that happened to me and what I learned. I am writing my story now, because the world is sinking rapidly into moral and political chaos and I know that the knowledge of a living, real God, a God of miracles may help others who are struggling as I was.

I dedicate this book to the glory of a living God who awakened in me a remembrance of His greatness and power.

I had a *"Burning Bush"* experience with God. I have witnessed a miracle from Him. On this basis I can bear a faithful and true witness that God lives and is real.

This is my story.

Nancy Goldberg Hilton
May 1, 2006
Salt Lake City, Utah, USA

CHAPTER 1

Birth and Career
(1946–1990)

> *Behold, the days come, saith the Lord, that I will make a new covenant with the house of Israel, and with the house of Judah: Not according to the covenant that I made with their fathers in the day that I took them by the hand to bring them out of the land of Egypt; which my covenant they brake, although I was an husband unto them, saith the Lord. [Jeremiah 31:31–32]*

JEWISH HERITAGE

I am a small Jewish child sitting in a synagogue listening to the Cantor singing our ancient Jewish songs. His tone was melodious and reassuring; his words inspiring. Then I listened to the rabbi speak words of praise to our one Eternal God. We rose and sang together the sacred prayer of the Jewish people, the Shema.

Shema Yisrael Adonai Eloheinu Adonai Echad
Hear, O Israel: the Lord our God, the Lord is One.

Barukh Shem kvod malhuto le'olam va-ed
Praised be His name whose glorious kingdom is forever and ever.

Then we all said together in Hebrew first and then in English:

And thou shalt love the Lord thy God with all thine heart and with all thy soul, and with all thy might.

And these words, which I command thee this day, shall be in thine heart:

And thou shalt teach them diligently unto thy children, and shalt talk of them when thou sittest in thine house, and when thou walkest by the way, and when thou liest down, and when thou risest up.

And thou shalt bind them for a sign upon thine hand, and they shall be as frontlets between thine eyes.

And thou shalt write them upon the posts of thy house, and on thy gates. [Deut. 6:5–9]

I remember, as a young child, feeling close to God every time I said these words. I looked around the synagogue. In the front of the room, stood our rabbi. Behind him covered with a curtain were the Torah scrolls. I sat quietly, feeling reassured and at peace with my surroundings.

I was born into a Jewish family in Baltimore, Maryland on November 25, 1946 and was raised by good parents, in a loving home. I felt protected and cared for. I have a wonderful older brother who now is the father of three children and five grandchildren.

My Childhood

As a young girl, I went to Hebrew School and was taught the stories of our ancient Jewish faith in God who opened the Red Sea and brought us out of Egypt. I was given instruction about a powerful God who provided miracles for our people and made a covenant with our father, Abraham (see Genesis 22:15–18). He was a God who gave instructions to ancient prophets who led and guided our Jewish nation.

I was taught the traditional Jewish prayers and songs and loved to sing them in our synagogue. But I always felt that there had to be more than this; more to know about this God whom we worshiped. What happened to this God? Where is he now? The God I learned about was an ancient God and all of his events and miracles happened a long time ago.

I was taught that God had no form or substance. That prophets had ceased to exist on the earth and that our counsel should now come from our rabbis and the center of Jewish life was in a synagogue not a temple. I was taught that if I followed the laws of God and our traditions I would maintain my connection with God. But what was this connection? Why did I need it? What was the meaning of Judaism?

As I grew older my need for God faded and thoughts of boy friends, parties and school work occupied my time. After all, who was God anyway? What did he have to do with me? To be Jewish meant dating Jewish boys and having only Jewish girl friends. It meant going to the synagogue twice per year during Rosh Hashanah (Jewish New Year) and Yom Kippur (the Day of Atonement). It also meant eating a Passover meal (Seder) once a year.

I realized that this God, a God of miracles, had abandoned us in our greatest times of national trial (the Holocaust and World War II). From this failure of God to protect us, I lost hope that there was a true and living God who could help me in this life. That God's promises were hollow and his covenant meaningless. He was not a living God that I could depend on. He was not real. So I abandoned my belief in Him and turned my back on thinking about Him or relying on Him. There were no more miracles. All that was left was to follow the traditions of my faith. Slowly my belief in a living God was smothered like a candle that once was lit with hope but later snuffed out leaving only smoke that is blown by the wind.

By hindsight, I now know that it was not God's failure; but our failure. We had rejected His prophets, abandoned many of His commandments and adopted the ways of the world.

One thing that I learned at an early age was to mistrust anyone not of my religion. Because my last name was Goldberg, I was labeled Jewish. Many times I was afraid and I felt like the world was against me. I remember an incident when I was ten years old. We had just moved to a new neighborhood and I wanted to play with the girls next door. When I knocked on their door, the girls who lived there came out and one said to me, "We cannot play with you because you killed Jesus Christ." I did not understand their meaning. Who was Jesus Christ anyway and why was he killed? I certainly had not hurt let alone killed anyone. But I heard the name of Jesus Christ used many times as I grew up, not in terms of love, but in terms of hate and persecution. I actually feared the name of Jesus Christ.

I was raised with values. I was taught to keep and follow the Ten Commandments (Exodus 20). I was also taught to be generous and kind. It was a mitzvah (blessing) to help others in need. In my childish mind, I thought everyone in the world also lived by these values. I was soon to learn otherwise.

Regardless of my lack of belief in God, I was still Jewish and planned to remain stalwart in this faith. I cannot tell you why I felt this way but I did. I had no desire to be Christian or any other religion. Being Jewish was a part of my life, my tradition and my values.

School and University

I graduated from high school in 1964 and decided to attend Boston University for my freshman year at college. I was separated from the shelter of my home and thrust into an alien environment filled with all kinds of people. I found out very quickly that I could not always trust people. They did not live by the Ten Commandments and in fact rarely gave them any thought. It was the 1960s, and personal standards were changing quickly. It was a difficult year. I learned to adapt to my new environment, and by the end of the year was enjoying myself and my new freedom from home.

My parents moved to Dallas, Texas during my freshman year in college, so I decided to transfer to the University of Texas in Austin for my sophomore year in 1965. I graduated in 1967, at the age of twenty, with a BS degree in Art.

CAREER AND MARRIAGE

I worked, part time, through the last two years of college as a secretary. I found out a degree in art was worth very little in the job market.

I moved to Dallas, Texas in 1967 and got my first full-time job as a secretary with an advertising agency. I thought this was a good compromise. I could use my skill as a secretary to make a living but visit the agency's art department to gain needed knowledge on how to become a professional artist. The advertising artists were very talented, and I enjoyed learning from them. However, there was another side to the advertising business that I did not like. I became aware of how business was done at this agency with long luncheons, alcohol, and other means of acquiring business. I was very uncomfortable in this environment, and after one year I decided to look for another job.

I found work as a secretary for a title insurance company in downtown Dallas, Texas. This work was fascinating, and I learned all that I could. There were strict rules set forth in doing this work, not only by the Texas State Board of Insurance but by the people who worked in the industry. It required a lot of technical skill and knowledge about real estate law, preparation of legal papers for transferring title, banking, and research into titles, working with all kinds of people including attorneys, surveyors, buyers, sellers, and real estate agents. It was never dull and I was always learning something new. It was a great challenge intellectually. I thrived in this environment. The work was hard but honest. I loved and respected the people I worked for. I was treated fairly and they always helped me learn the business. I worked long hours at the office and then more at home on the weekends. My job became my life. I continued to work in this industry for many years.

In 1968, I married a Jewish man whom I had met at the University of Texas. He did not want to have children, and I wanted to postpone having a family until I had achieved my career goal.

So we both worked and eventually, after many years, became financially successful. By 1984, I was a branch manager of a major title insurance company in Dallas, Texas. I loved my work and had great success in business. My clients were fantastic, and the work very challenging and exciting. Success, to me, resulted in being able to purchase a large home, two cars, the clothes we needed for our careers, and other items of comfort. But the more we had the more we wanted. We purchased a vacation home on the coast and stocked it with furniture, and had an extra car. Then we bought a boat. Soon much of our time was spent taking care of these extra things. I remember thinking, I am not enjoying these things, I am owned by them! We would go to our vacation home to clean it and take care of it. Then it was time to leave. We could only take off a few days at a time so the enjoyment of this place never happened. But it was fun to be able to say—"Oh, we are successful; we own another home and cars. Look at us, see what we have!"

I did not have much of a religious life. I felt obligated to go to the synagogue two times a year during the High Holy Days, and I was obedient in doing this. The Day of Atonement is the way the Jewish people seek forgiveness of their sins. I fasted for an entire day and prayed in the synagogue and asked for forgiveness. This was done by reading out of a prayer book and listening to our rabbi. I tried to feel something when I went to synagogue during these important religious holidays but did not feel forgiven nor did I feel close to God. What I liked best about these holidays was the feeling of being part of a Jewish nation all talking together about our ancient God. I still had a yearning, buried deep inside of me, to understand and connect with God even if I were not religious or very observant. But how would this ever be possible?

Every Passover, I would hear again the story of Moses and the miracles of God in leading the children of Israel out of Egypt. During Passover we would open the door for the Prophet Elijah and have a cup of wine for him and a place reserved at the table. I never understood who Elijah was and why we did this, but it was tradition so we did it. I love the story of Passover and especially when our family celebrated it together. As an adult I viewed this as a tradition. But I can remember as a very small child that it had greater meaning for me as we talked about God and His miracles. I can still see my father at the head of our table, beautifully set, speaking Hebrew and telling this ancient story. It is a precious memory for me.

Many of my Christian friends tried to tell me about Jesus Christ. But no amount of effort by them convinced me to visit their churches or listen to their doctrine. I was Jewish and that was all I needed to know. I would say to my Christian friends, "I have a direct relationship with God. I don't have to go through anybody else, like Jesus Christ." But these words had no meaning as I did not understand what they were talking about nor did I have any meaningful relationship with God that I knew of.

The year 1991 was pivotal. My marriage was failing and very difficult. I wanted to leave my husband but did not have the courage to do anything about it. I had the trappings of success by the world's standards, but inside I was empty and afraid. I hated to go home at night and worked late hours. I needed some help. I went to a marriage counselor, but that was not the answer. I never considered seeking help from a rabbi or any other religious person.

I would ask myself, "What more was there to life? Was this all there is? Why was I feeling so alone and empty inside? How could I feel better?" I knew some people filled up their emptiness with worldly activities that were not good for them. I did not smoke, take drugs, or drink alcohol; and I would never start. I knew that this was not what I wanted. It was not the answer.

Thoughts of suicide coursed through my mind quite often. Our vacation home was on a canal, and we had a dock that led out in the water. I would sit on the end of this dock in the evening, and these thoughts would come into my mind. *If you go into the water and drown you will not feel this emptiness inside of you anymore. You will be free from pain.* I rejected these thoughts over and over.

How could I even think such thoughts? I had everything. What more could I ask for? I would sometimes drive home, after work, and not even remember driving. There were so many thoughts running through my mind—so many mental conversations that I thought I was going crazy. In hopes of diverting these recurring thoughts, I started to do my artwork again. I took watercolor lessons and painted every night. I joined the watercolor society and met a new group of people. This hobby helped me and diverted my negative thoughts.

I felt like a woman going through a revolving door. I would take on one personality going into my office as an efficient business woman and another going home as a subservient housewife. Somewhere inside that revolving door, I forgot who I was. But I chose this life-style and did not think that I had the strength to change it. If I changed it, what would I change it into? I felt trapped.

CHAPTER 2

My Burning Bush Experience
(1991–1995)

> And the angel of the Lord appeared unto him [Moses] in a flame of fire out of the midst of a bush and he looked, and behold, the bush burned with fire, and the bush was not consumed . . . And when the Lord saw that he turned aside to see, God called unto him out of the midst of the bush, and said, Moses, Moses. And he said, Here am I . . . . Moreover he said, I am the God of thy father, the God of Abraham, the God of Isaac, and the God of Jacob. And Moses hid his face; for he was afraid to look upon God. [Exodus 3:2, 4 and 6]

SEARCHING FOR ANSWERS

During this time of my life, I took a hard look at who I was and what I had achieved. My success in business was wonderful. Our title insurance office worked on commercial transactions such as land development, construction, and sale of apartments, office buildings, and shopping centers. I attribute this success to my loyal and wonderful clients, my employers who taught me so much, hard working and capable employees, and my own work ethic as well. I loved my work, its excitement and challenge. I tried hard to anticipate any problems that could arise and always went the extra mile for my clients. I was honest in my dealings, and my clients knew that they could trust me. This work was very complex and detailed. I had the ability to see the big picture and explain complex issues in a simple understandable way.

I remember how we would gather around our conference room table and fill it from one end to the other with legal documents. We were working together to close a complex development of land and buildings, and it took many people to work together to accomplish it. I was able to understand how the flow should go—what had to take place—the critical title, legal, and accounting information that had to be assembled and finalized. The more complex the closing was, the better I liked it. This ability was a gift and had come to me after many years of experience and hard work.

But I still had many personal problems and felt like I needed help from somewhere. At night as I tried to work through my problems, a thought came to me. Maybe I could say a prayer? I remember as a child I felt comforted when I said the Shema. So every night I would say this Jewish prayer before I went to sleep. I realize now I was trying to reach out to God in the only way I knew.

My mother called me one day and told me about a book-author luncheon that she was in charge of to raise money for the National Council of Jewish Women. One of the authors wrote a book that she wanted me to read. So she mailed it to me.

This book was about a psychiatrist who hypnotized people to find out about their past lives. It was his theory that we lived before and that we had traumas in our past lives that affected our current lives. I thought this book was very interesting. So I read more books on this subject. Thus, I started to learn about the psychic world—a world of wizards, mediums, psychics, Ouija boards, and meditation. I went to a psychic who told me things about myself that astonished me. How could she know these things? There must be some truth to this spirit world stuff. So I read more.

I read about people who had visits from "spiritual guides" that were angels in the form of men. These spirit guides were like guardian angels who help us when the need arose. I read that each of us has a guardian angel, or spirit guide, to help and direct our lives. But we must seek for these guides and ask them to help us.

I read more books and realized how popular this subject was. One book was about a man who received information on how to heal people. There were many documented cases of people that he did heal using the information he received from the world of the dead. There were movies and television shows that also dealt with this inviting subject. I was pulled into this world not really understanding what I was doing or the consequences.

I started to meditate and go to psychic fairs. This really was a big business, and many people made a living from it.

I was fascinated by a book about a woman's spiritual journey— how her spirit separated from her body and soared into space. I wanted to try and do this but was afraid. She talked about being surrounded by white light and the peace she felt. I wanted this peace in my life too. I wanted some answers on what would be best for me. What direction should my life take? Why wasn't I happy? Was I just being a spoiled brat, not appreciating all I had? Maybe I could get my answers from my spiritual guide if I could find him?

My Spiritual Battle 1992

So here I was in the year 1992 praying to a God that I did not know or understand, in Hebrew each night, and also meditating and seeking for a spiritual guide as well. I was setting up the perfect spiritual battle ready for me to step into. I did not expect what was coming.

I needed some relief from the stress of my failed marriage and the emptiness I was feeling. My mother called and invited me to come with her and my father on a vacation to Arizona and Nevada. As an adult, I had never had a vacation separate from my husband, but I decided it was time to venture forth. This was the perfect solution, I thought, to get away from my problems.

My parents reserved a time-share apartment in Arizona, and we would stay there for a few days. Then we planned a tourist visit to Rainbow Bridge, a huge natural bridge of reddish sandstone at Lake Powell. After that we would go to Las Vegas and then home. It sounded wonderful, so I accepted their invitation.

I went early to Arizona and met my cousin before my parents arrived. We planned to go to the Grand Canyon. I had never been there before. I remember the first look at this magnificent sight. It really was awe inspiring. After looking around, I settled down in a beautiful spot, took out my paints, and started watercolor painting the scenery before me of the Grand Canyon. I remember how happy I felt to be away from Dallas and my problems. I was free and excited. But, I knew that this was only temporary.

My cousin was also involved in finding out about things of the spirit and knew about the psychic world. She and I talked about my need for some type of spiritual help. I really yearned for something to happen from the spirit world that would give me some guidance.

After our visit to the Grand Canyon, my cousin drove me to the place where I met my parents. I felt wonderful and spent a lovely day with my family. Then events happened there that would shape the future course of my life.

During my visit to this vacation place, I sought for a way to connect with my spiritual guide. I did not realize that there were evil spirits in addition to good ones, and that the results of this quest might open spiritual doors which I could not close. I expected a peaceful journey surrounded by white light traveling through space and time.

I did have a spiritual experience when I attempted to do this that resulted in a great spiritual battle with the forces of evil. As I innocently asked for a spiritual guide to help me in life, the reality of a vast spirit world became apparent to me, and I realized that I was ill-equipped to handle what was happening. What I felt was a huge evil force that was beyond my comprehension. I can tell you that evil beings are real. They are not cartoon characters or frightening creatures in movies. They are real and powerful, and I was afraid!

I returned to my parent's apartment after this happened and tried to rest. As soon as I closed my eyes, I had what you could say were vivid nightmares. Sleep left me for fear that I would not awaken. I was sick to my stomach and could not eat. I was like an innocent child facing a mighty force that I did not understand. This was not a drug, food, or alcohol related event, as I never partook of those substances. It was real!

I dared not explain this to my parents and have never talked about it to them. They knew something had happened, but did not ask. We left the next day to visit my cousin. I was exhausted. Thoughts of my death coursed through my mind as I continued through this strange world of darkness. I yearned for something or someone to help me, but who or what?

If I thought I had problems before, this new event just compounded them enormously. Obviously, I had not made a good choice.

MY BURNING BUSH—MY MIRACLE AT RAINBOW BRIDGE 1992

After a brief overnight visit with my cousin, we drove to Page, Arizona for a boat trip to Rainbow Bridge. This two and one-half hour boat ride started at Wahweep Marina. I felt nauseous and had eaten very little in two days.

I had always wanted to see Rainbow Bridge. For some reason, I was very anxious to get there. In fact, I felt a sense of urgency. The day was cloudy and rainy when we started out. I was afraid that the boat would not go if it were raining; however, the rain soon disappeared and the sun came out. The trip was magnificent as the lake is filled with huge red rocks jutting out of the water.

The boat turned into a side channel and finally arrived at the dock leading to the bridge. We were told there was a one-half mile hike to the bridge and that we must return in 45 minutes. I was the first one off the boat and walked quickly across the long dock to the sandy path that led to the bridge. The first sight of this magnificent bridge that spans this side canyon was thrilling. I was amazed at its height and beauty. But most of all I was happy to feel a sense of peace which came upon me. I felt safe here.

I walked under the bridge and up the small hill next to it. I found a place to sit and rest. I looked around and saw hundreds of people from the excursion boats milling around. I thought to myself, *It would be nice to be here alone.* I was so tired and soon fell asleep.

Rainbow Bridge, Glen Canyon National Recreation Area, Utah National Park Service Digital Image Archives, used with permission.

When I awoke, I felt water on my face. I stood up and realized that I was in a rain storm. It began raining harder, and I was getting soaked. I looked around and could not see any other person. I was alone just as I had hoped for!

I walked down the slope toward the base of the bridge.

As I walked under the bridge, I heard one loud clap of thunder! It shook the earth.

The sound coursed through me, and I felt a great change enter my whole being. My mind was instantly opened to understand the things of God. All my feelings of darkness and evil left me. I instantly accepted the reality of God's being. I knew that His Son was Jesus Christ, a person whose love extended out to me at this time of personal crisis. He was truly my Savior at that moment as all thoughts of my past trials faded, and my heart was filled with wonder, compassion, peace, and love. This experience was brief, but its effect on my life will last forever.

I stood in the rain, not feeling cold or wet, but feeling free from darkness and at peace. I was filled with a spirit of joy that words cannot describe. I felt a strong and powerful connection to God and His Son Jesus Christ. I remember feeling one with Them and everything around me. It was as if our world was in perfect unison, and everything was in order. God was at the helm.

I said out loud, "You are baptizing me here at Rainbow Bridge." What strange words for me to say as I never thought about baptism except in terms of persecution for the Jewish people. But now, I felt glorious and protected.

I was in the presence of a God of miracles as one was happening to me at that moment. God was alive! He communicated with me. He touched my heart and soul. I discovered miracles had not ceased, nor should they ever. I learned about His existence and His Son Jesus Christ. The God of Abraham, Isaac, and Jacob was the same God whom I felt at that moment. This experience to me was sacred and wondrous. I was so grateful to God for helping me. I wept.

The Lord, Jesus Christ, gave me a new life. He reached out to me in love and awakened in me a suppressed memory of who He was. I did not fully understand nor did I ask why this knowledge was given to me. I was content to feel a connection to God once again. I knew that this connection had always been there but the knowledge of Him and His Beloved Son had been hidden. Now it was flowering and blooming, and I wanted it to continue.

I looked to my left and saw a gigantic, towering waterfall that pounded on the ground next to me. I thought, *This is the power and might of God.* I looked to my right and saw many small waterfalls and thought of the beauty and gentleness of God. I looked behind me and was surprised to see two people standing there looking at me. They had an old-fashioned tripod camera. Their presence did not concern me. I wondered if they were angels. But if they were mortal and had taken my picture, I would love to see it. What a precious moment this had been.

I did not want to leave this place. But soon, I felt, I must return to the boat. I reluctantly started down the path toward the excursion boat. I saw ahead of me two enormous waterfalls blocking my path. I also saw two men maneuvering their way under the waterfalls toward me. I recognized them from our boat. They had come looking for me. One of them took my hand, and together we ducked under the large waterfall. I felt the sting of sand from the cascading water.

We all stopped and looked back at Rainbow Bridge. It was a magnificent sight standing as a testimony to me of what I had experienced there. The sun was coming out, and I could see it reflected on every drop of rain as if I had a special curtain made up of rainbow colors framing the bridge before me. Finally, the rain stopped and the curtain disappeared. I turned my back to the bridge and walked to the boat.

My mother said, "You have kept us waiting." I replied, "Be glad that I am here." I had been gone for two hours. But to me, I had been gone for just a moment. In that moment, my whole life had changed. God had touched my soul.

I put on a warm, dry sweater and sat down as we pulled away from the dock toward our home port. I did not say a word to anyone. But the passengers were so kind and offered me food and something to drink. They were concerned. I could still feel the peace and love that had just washed through my body. I did not want to let go of that feeling. What I had experienced was sacred and special. I had to think about it.

I thought of Moses as he stood before the *burning bush*. Did Moses feel like this? His life changed from that time forth, and so did mine. I felt a kinship to him.

Most of all, I thought of Jesus Christ. Before this event, I never thought about Him except as an enemy to the Jewish people and to me. In His name evil men killed and tortured many people, including my ancestors. But now, I knew differently. I only felt love and compassion from Him. Could this be the same person that the "Christians" had been talking about?

That night I finally slept peacefully. I had no nightmares. I was quiet inside. My soul was at rest.

In looking back at these events, I realize that Satan's door to the spiritual world is a poor substitute for the reality of God's inspiration and glory. Satan's way leads to fear and destruction, while God's way leads to happiness, freedom, and love. I also knew that the God of miracles still existed and so did His Son Jesus Christ, whom I realized was the promised Messiah of Judah. I knew that God continues to communicate with us. I did not hear a voice with my ears, but my mind had been opened to His truth.

God gave me a spiritual gift that day. I had been asking and asking Him for guidance, not knowing that I was reaching out to Him with my prayer, my shema. I know that I was humbly seeking the truth, and I received it. How marvelous to know God lives and His Son is Jesus Christ, the Messiah.

The next day we drove to Las Vegas. My parents had arranged for us to attend a magic show that evening, and I was looking forward to seeing it. The show was wonderful. But it paled in comparison to the reality of a true miracle from God.

Afterward, I put some coins in a slot machine, but the machine would not accept the money. I put the coins in a few more machines, and again the money would drop through to the bottom. I understood that I should not gamble, so I stopped and have never gambled since.

When I returned to Dallas, my husband could tell that I had changed. I felt quiet and peaceful. Nothing that he said could harm me anymore. I told my husband about my experiences on my vacation with my parents, and it scared him.

Because of this, I had the strength to find an apartment and move out of my house. After twenty-five years of marriage, it finally ended in divorce. I thought I would celebrate the day it finally happened, but instead I quietly cried.

My Search for the Truth
about Jesus Christ

Now I was on a journey of knowledge to see if I could bring together information I would receive from the Christian community about God and Jesus Christ and combine it with ancient Judaism. My hope was to find a way to connect or link all the facets together.

So how do I start my search? The first thing I did was to purchase a Bible with both the Old and New Testaments. As a child, in Hebrew school, I read parts of the five books of Moses.

I was surprised to discover that the New Testament was also written by Jews. Peter, James, John, Matthew, Mark, and Paul were all Jewish. I never knew this before, as I had never read or owned a New Testament. Jesus Christ was also Jewish, and now I have the book that gave the details of His life. This is important information. I started to read the New Testament and learn about Jesus Christ.

I was thinking about the words of the Jewish prayer, the Shema. I was astonished when I came across the familiar words in the New Testament. Jesus was asked by the Jewish scribe,

> Which is the first commandment of all?
> And Jesus answered him, The first of all the commandments is, Hear, O Israel; The Lord our God is one Lord:

And thou shalt love the Lord thy God with all thy heart, and with all thy soul, and with all thy mind, and with all thy strength: this is the first commandment.

And the second is like, namely this, Thou shalt love thy neighbour as thyself. There is none other commandment greater than these. [Mark 12:28–31]

These sacred words are in both the New and the Old Testament, and Jesus Christ said it was the first commandment. This was an important connection for me. Here was a link between the sacred prayer of the Jewish people and Jesus Christ. I always felt that Judaism and Christianity were entirely different, but here were links between the two that might have been lost or forgotten.

I kept reading the New Testament, but still did not have a clear understanding about Jesus Christ and what He did for us. Why did He die? What was the meaning of His atoning sacrifice? Why was it important that He overcame death? I read about His Resurrection. What did the sacrifice of Jesus Christ have to do with me?

In my Hebrew school I had learned that we do not live after death. We are remembered by our good deeds and our family but our lives ended at death. When I lost a loved one, I was profoundly sad because I did not think I would ever see him or her again. But now I was reading about Jesus Christ who overcame death and was seen by hundreds of people after His resurrection. The Apostles touched His hands and the marks of the nails. He ate food. He had a glorious body and walked, talked and taught His apostles for forty days. Then they saw Him ascend to heaven (see Luke 24:51). I read with interest these words:

All things must be fulfilled which were written in the law of Moses, and in the prophets, and in the psalms, concerning me . . . .

And said unto them, Thus it is written, and thus it behoved Christ to suffer, and to rise from the dead the third day:

And that repentance and remission of sins should be preached in his name among all nations, beginning at Jerusalem. [Luke 24:44, 46–47]

But what does it mean for me that Jesus Christ rose from the dead? What is repentance and remission of sin?

I learned that the Pharisees, in ancient Judaism, believed in the doctrine of immortality and resurrection of the body and the existence of angels and spirits and that some sects of Judaism today also believe in the literal coming of a Messiah. I was never taught these doctrines in my youth. I realized that I had a lot to learn about Judaism as well as Christianity.

So what about the Christians? How do they put into practice the teachings of Jesus Christ? Can they explain all of this unfamiliar doctrine to me? Can they tell me about Jesus Christ and His purpose?

I learned about Judaism in Hebrew school, so I assumed I could learn about Jesus Christ in a Christian church. But which church should I attend? I opened the yellow pages of the telephone book in Dallas, Texas and saw listed page after page of Christian churches. How can there be so many churches? Didn't Jesus have one church? Which one was the right one?

Visiting Christian Churches

When I thought of Jesus Christ, I felt love and friendship. I was anxious to learn more about Him from the Christian churches. I had changed in such a profound way after my miraculous experience. When I concentrated on Him, I could feel His love and peace as a part of my everyday life. My voice became softer. I was quieter and more reflective. So I was looking forward to learning more.

When my friends found out that I wanted to go to church, they invited me to theirs. I felt very strange walking into a church. The first one I attended preached hatred against the Jews because they killed Christ. I was horrified at his words and was very offended. There were small children in attendance, and likely they would repeat these words just as I used to hear them so long ago. This was not a good beginning for my search. He made it sound as if every modern Jewish person was responsible for the killing of Jesus Christ. He totally overlooked the fact that the New Testament, upon which he based his talk, was also written by Jews. Jesus Christ and the Apostles were Jewish. I thought, doesn't this preacher know that Jesus Christ is about love and forgiveness. He is real, He lives! They should be talking about the joy and love He can bring to our lives. This preacher would not have a job in his Church if it were not for the death of Jesus Christ. Why isn't he talking about the love of God rather than spreading hatred?

I asked my friend, who invited me to this church, to talk to her preacher about my feelings. His response to her was that his father, who was also a preacher, had always taught this doctrine, and so did he. He had never considered it would be offensive to modern Jews. I never returned to his church.

Over the next four years, I was invited by many wonderful and caring people, who truly believe in Jesus Christ, to visit their churches; but I did not feel that any of their churches were right for me. Everywhere I went, I felt uncomfortable. I was a Jew walking in a Christian world that could not relate to me, nor me to them. Why was this so?

I always asked about Jesus Christ. I was told over and over again. Just let Him into your heart and you are saved. I asked them to explain what they meant by that phrase, but they could not. This statement did not make sense to me. It was not logical. Was it enough to just believe in Jesus Christ? Some told about grace, others about works, and both argued about it. They told me that I was saved without having to do anything at all. I asked them, "Saved from what?" I understood that we were saved from sin. But how can you be saved from sin if you keep sinning and do not repent, change, and keep the commandments? I know of several people that go to church on Sunday and do terrible things during the week. I was getting more and more confused. I thought, *How can you be saved and ignore the commandments of God and the teachings of Jesus Christ?*

Some churches had rock bands and played loud popular music. At one of them, the preacher handed out a paper when we entered his church, and had us fill in the blanks from his sermon as to his philosophy of life; and then he departed from the stage. This was a popular church, but it was insulting to my intelligence.

I found it interesting that I would ask the same question at many of the churches I attended, even churches of the same denomination, and always got different answers. Each one had their own doctrine, traditions, and rituals; but where was the power of God? I was told miracles and revelation ceased with the death of the ancient Apostles. Many of them never discussed Jesus Christ. When they talked about Him they usually taught me about His death and suffering but little about His glorious Resurrection. They talked about His pain but not about the Atonement and the doctrine of repentance. They talked about hatred against the Jews but not His love and forgiveness. It was the churches that caused my problem, not the people.

As I traveled from one church to another, I entered a journey of confusion. I met so many truly believing and faithful people. However, it seemed to me that the traditions of each church were set in an immovable pattern. I was told this is how it has always been done. I heard so often, "I am Catholic," "I am Greek Orthodox," "I am Baptist," "I am . . . ." It was as if we all wore our religions like a badge protecting us from learning more and separating us from each other.

They were silent about the contributions of the Jews to Christianity. It was totally ignored and actually forgotten. I found each church was separate and apart. But I knew that we should all be one. Paul said, "One Lord, one faith and one baptism" (Ephesians 4:5). Where was this oneness, this feeling of unity of purpose with our God and His Son, Jesus Christ?

Many of the people that I met in church expressed a desire to know more about God and Jesus Christ. They wanted a sign, a miracle or some proof of God's reality.

All the churches were decorated with frightful images of Jesus such as the cross, the crucifix, and icons. I was not comfortable among these surroundings, as I had been brought up in the Jewish faith with the commandment, "Thou shalt not make unto thee any graven image, or any likeness of anything that is in heaven above" (Exodus 20:4). I saw precious souls talking to and kissing these images. I thought, *I hope they haven't relegated Jesus Christ to a picture on the wall or a figurine nailed to a cross instead of a living being.*

Occasionally, I attended Friday night services at the Jewish synagogue. I went quite often as I felt comfortable there, but I knew that Jesus Christ was not part of their belief. I now knew that He was the Messiah, and maybe someday the Jewish people would know this also and feel the same love for Him that I felt.

After my experiences with the many forms of Christian religion I encountered over four years, I finally decided to give up. No one had the answers that I sought. None of them expressed a belief in a living, powerful God—a God of miracles. They did not believe in inspiration or revelation. I had this incredible experience at Rainbow Bridge. I knew God was real and I knew that His Son was Jesus Christ. That was enough for me.

My quest had failed. I did not feel, not once, in any of the churches I visited the same feeling of the spirit that I felt at Rainbow Bridge. Shouldn't I have felt that same feeling if I were in the right church?

CHAPTER 3

Met the Latter-day Saints
(1995–1996)

Whom shall he teach knowledge? And whom shall he make to understand doctrine? . . . For precept must be upon precept, precept upon precept; line upon line, line upon line; here a little, and there a little. [Isaiah 28:9–10]

And in that day shall the deaf hear the words of the book, and the eyes of the blind shall see out of obscurity, and out of darkness. [Isaiah 29:18]

They also that erred in spirit shall come to understanding, and they that murmured shall learn doctrine. [Isaiah 29:24]

THE BOOK OF MORMON

It was the year 1995. By this time I had started my own title insurance company. It was a risk to start this business, but soon proved to be successful.

I flew from Dallas to Houston, Texas to meet some people about future title insurance business. I told my business contact about my belief in Jesus Christ. He asked if I would accept a book to read. I told him, "All right." He handed me a copy of the Book of Mormon. He told me that he was a member of The Church of Jesus Christ of Latter-day Saints, known as the Mormons. He explained, briefly, the nature of this book and marked a few passages he thought I would like to read.

I started to read the following from the Book of Mormon while I was on the airplane flying back to Dallas, Texas. "The Book of Mormon is a volume of holy scripture comparable to the Bible. It is a record of God's dealings with the ancient inhabitants of the Americas and contains, as does the Bible, the fullness of the everlasting gospel" (Introduction to the Book of Mormon).

As I read the words in the Book of Mormon, a sense of peace and love filled my heart again. This book was fascinating. I read with great interest the title page:

> Written to . . . Jew and Gentile—Written by way of commandment, and also by the spirit of prophecy and of revelation . . . To come forth by the gift and power of God . . . .
>
> . . . That they may know the covenants of the Lord, that they are not cast off forever—And also to the convincing of the Jew and Gentile that Jesus is the Christ. [Book of Mormon, Title Page]

Then I started to read the first chapter of the Book of Mormon entitled "The First Book of Nephi," and this is what it says:

> For it came to pass in the commencement of the first year of the reign of Zedekiah, king of Judah, (my father, Lehi, having dwelt at Jerusalem in all his days); and in that same year there came many prophets, prophesying unto the people that they must repent, or the great city Jerusalem must be destroyed.
>
> Wherefore it came to pass that my father, Lehi, as he went forth prayed unto the Lord, yea, even with all his heart, in behalf of his people.
>
> And it came to pass as he prayed unto the Lord, there came a pillar of fire and dwelt upon a rock before him; and he saw and heard much; and because of the things which he saw and heard he did quake and tremble exceedingly.
>
> . . . . He was carried away in a vision, even that he saw the heavens open, and he thought he saw God sitting upon his throne, surrounded with numberless concourses of angels in the attitude of singing and praising their God." [1 Nephi 1:4–6, 8]

To me, reading this book was like looking at the history of the Jewish nation in a new light. One that included the inspiration of a living God that continued to strive with his people and communicate through prophets in the new world. The life of Lehi and his family is described in detail as he preached to the people in Jerusalem and then fled for his life to a promised land in America. Lehi lived in the year 600 B.C., at the same time as the Prophet Jeremiah.

I found it very interesting to learn that Lehi also took with him, to the new world, the "plates of brass" which contained "the five books of Moses, which gave an account of the creation of the world, and also of Adam and Eve, who were our first parents; And also a record of the Jews from the beginning , even down to the commencement of the reign of Zedekiah, king of Judah; and also the prophecies of the holy prophets, from the beginning even down to the commencement of the reign of Zedekiah; and also many prophecies which have been spoken by the mouth of Jeremiah" (1 Nephi 5:11–13).

These plates also contained Lehi's genealogy, so he knew that he was a descendant of Joseph, son of Jacob who was sold into Egypt.

Lehi understood the importance of these plates of brass and that they "should go forth unto all nations, kindreds, tongues, and people who were of his seed" (1 Nephi 5:18). This way the records could be searched by Lehi's descendants, and the commandments of the Lord would be preserved in the new land. Lehi, his family, and many of his descendants kept the law of Moses in America—including bloody sacrifices, synagogues, and building temples.

As I read further, my mind started to open up to a new truth, one that would consume my thoughts. This book described the history of the Jews, linked it to Jesus Christ, the Messiah, and then brought it forward in time to a glorious gathering and plan of God.

The question that came to my mind was this—I had heard the term Messiah in my Jewish religion, but never understood who this should be or what He should do for us. Could it be that our prophets through the ages actually preached about the coming of Jesus Christ as our Messiah who would come to earth as the Son of God and overcome death and sin? Was what Lehi preached in Jerusalem and in America the same as he and other prophets preached from the beginning? Was that why he was threatened and had to flee for his life from Jerusalem? Nephi, the son of Lehi said that the Messiah would come 600 years from the time that his father left Jerusalem (1 Nephi 10:4). That would be the time that Jesus Christ was born in Jerusalem. So, the question is, was the fullness of the gospel preached in Jerusalem as Lehi said it was?

Why had this information been lost? What happened to it? Is this why the Book of Mormon was preserved so that we, as Jews, could understand what information had been lost from the Old Testament? Was the Book of Mormon referred to in Isaiah 29:11–12? "And in that day shall the deaf hear the *words of the book,* and the eyes of the blind shall see out of obscurity, and out of darkness" (Isaiah 29:18, emphasis added).

I found the book of Isaiah is quoted extensively in Second Nephi of the Book of Mormon. Isaiah also had prophesied about the coming of the Messiah. "Therefore the Lord himself shall give you a sign—Behold, a virgin shall conceive, and bear a son, and shall call his name Immanuel" (Isaiah 7:14; 2 Nephi 17:14).

Maybe this Book of Mormon was the link I was looking for to bridge the Old and New Testaments; linking Judaism and Jesus Christ.

The Houston business associate came to Dallas the following week. I had so many questions to ask him.

I will never forget that day! I asked him, "Who was Jesus Christ? What was His purpose? Did I have a purpose on the earth? What happened after I died?" This kindly man explained, over several hours, the answers to my questions. He said he "*knew* the answers." I said, "How do you know the answers are true?" He told me he "knew the answers were true from the Holy Spirit of God." He said he "would have some missionaries come and teach me if I wanted to learn more."

But most important of all, was how I felt. I felt, once again, a strong connection to God as I listened to Him. It was the same feeling I had at Rainbow Bridge. I decided to find out about his church.

I continued to read the Book of Mormon with increasing interest. I also read the story of Joseph Smith, a modern prophet. When he was a young man he wanted to know which church to join, which one had the true doctrine of Jesus Christ. He decided to follow the council of James in the New Testament "If any of you lack wisdom, let him ask of God, that giveth to all men liberally, and upbraideth not; and it shall be given him" (James 1:5). So early in the spring of the year 1820, Joseph Smith, after prayer, received a glorious vision of God the Father and Jesus Christ, the Son:

> It was on the morning of a beautiful, clear day, early in the spring of eighteen hundred and twenty . . .

> I kneeled down and began to offer up the desires of my heart to God. I had scarcely done so, when immediately I was seized upon by some power which entirely overcame me, and had such an astonishing influence . . . that I could not speak. Thick darkness gathered around me, and it seemed to me for a time as if I were doomed to sudden destruction.

> But, exerting all my powers to call upon God to deliver me out of the power of this enemy which had seized upon me, and at the very moment when I was ready to sink into despair and abandon myself to destruction—not to an imaginary ruin, but to the power of some actual being from the unseen world, who had such marvelous power as I had never before felt in any being—just at this moment of great alarm, I saw a pillar of light exactly over my head, above the brightness of the sun, which descended gradually until it fell upon me.

> It no sooner appeared than I found myself delivered from the enemy which held me bound. When the light rested upon me I saw two Personages, whose brightness and glory defy all description, standing above me in the air. One of them spake unto me, calling me by name and said, pointing to the other—This is My Beloved Son. Hear Him!

> . . . I asked the Personages who stood above me in the light, which of all the sects was right . . . and which I should join.

I was answered that I must join none of them, for they were all wrong; and the Personage who addressed me said that all their creeds were an abomination in his sight; and those professors were all corrupt; that: "they draw near to me with their lips, but their hearts are far from me, they teach for doctrines the commandments of men, having a form of godliness, but they deny the power thereof. [Joseph Smith History 1:14–19]

I could certainly relate to his story. Like young Joseph, I too had been on a quest to find out the truth of the gospel and had gone to many churches. I had also experienced a spiritual battle and a glorious miracle of God. In my case, I did not see the physical presence of God or His Son like Joseph Smith did, but the impression it left on my mind was clear and personal. It took great faith and courage for Joseph to walk into a grove of trees and ask God what he should do. What marvelous revelations followed this event! Now I also knew that God and Jesus Christ have tangible bodies. What rejoicing I felt in my soul. I believed that Joseph Smith told the truth.

LEARNING THE FIRST PRINCIPLES OF THE GOSPEL

Two weeks later I received a call from two young, twenty-year-old, missionaries who said they could teach me some lessons about the Church. We set a date and time to meet at their church building. I wanted to see their church building. When I did, there were no crucifixes which emphasized the death of Christ, no candles, bells, incense, money boxes, or icons on the walls. There was no cross on the roof. In fact it was a plain building with no pretense or adornments. I liked that.

The missionaries explained that there were six lessons and gave me an outline of what they covered. I remember that the fourth one taught about the plan of salvation and life after death. I asked them to teach me that one first. But they refused, saying that all the knowledge

I would receive would be built line upon line, so I had to start at the beginning.

I would see if what I learned from this church would clear up my questions that I had after my four-year search. They certainly had my attention for two reasons. One was the Book of Mormon that I was reading, and the other was the spiritual feeling that I had when I read this book and when I was listening to the doctrines taught to me by these missionaries.

The basic message from The Church of Jesus Christ of Latter-day Saints was the *Restoration* in modern times of the ancient gospel of Jesus Christ. I was told that I would learn the true gospel of Jesus Christ. That it has been brought back in its fullness just like it was during the time when Jesus Christ was on the earth including all the gifts of the Spirit. The Church had a living, modern prophet and twelve Apostles. They had the power and authority of the priesthood, both Aaronic and Melchizedek. I was anxious to start learning.

But I had another goal. To me any knowledge that I received about God and Jesus Christ had to include ancient Judaism and Jesus Christ, as the Messiah. I felt like Judaism just stopped in its progression and that maybe I would discover that it was completed in the Restoration.

I knew that some of the elements, links or fulfillment of Judaism I was searching for must be:

- A true and living God
- The Messiah was Jesus Christ, the Son of God
- Priesthood power and authority
- Temple
- Miracles
- The Holy Spirit
- Repentance and baptism

I explained this to the missionaries. They were a bit overwhelmed with all my questions, so I was invited to one of the member's home to learn the gospel lessons with both the missionaries and members present. I soon learned that there were more books to read other than the Bible and the Book of Mormon. There was also the Doctrine and Covenants and the Pearl of Great Price which contained the book of Moses and the book of Abraham. If I read from all of these sources, I might eventually understand the big picture of the gospel that I was seeking. They explained to me that many plain and precious things had been lost or omitted from the Bible, and through the Restoration of the gospel many of these lost items were available to us again.

Learning to Pray

Before they taught me the first lesson, the missionaries asked if it were all right to say a prayer I said, "All right." One of the missionaries said the prayer. I was so astonished because this was not a memorized prayer, but one said from his heart. The words were beautiful, personal, and specific. I asked them to say another prayer, so I could learn how to pray myself. This was something so new to me, as I never knew that we could actually ask God questions or thank Him for blessings and receive an answer. I wrote down how to say a personal prayer. It is not difficult, but takes faith to try it. First, I address God as my Heavenly Father for I am His child. Second, I thank Him for my blessings and list them. Third, I ask specific questions for specific blessings or needs, and then I end in the name of Jesus Christ, amen. They told me that all prayer in the Church is like this and that I should pray at least twice a day, once in the morning and once in the evening. But actually God is available twenty-four hours a day, seven days a week, so I can talk to Him at any time. The key they said was that I had to ask! Then I had to wait for an answer or be aware later how God would answer me, so I could thank Him. When this would happen it would build my faith.

This was such a new concept to me. I was delighted. Of course, it made perfect sense. I learned that God is my Heavenly Father and that I was His child. I would never talk to my father on the earth with memorized phrases. I would be specific in talking to him. It was no different with my Heavenly Father. I think our Heavenly Father is tired of hearing us repeat the same phrases in prayer to Him all the time.

When I was investigating Christian churches prior to this time, one minister told me that God already knew what we needed, so we did not have to ask. But I realized now that I have free agency and God will not violate my free agency and force something on me, so I have to ask Him for help. Then He could do what was best for me. One was an active and the other a passive prayer. This way made more sense to me. I was the one responsible for my own life, my own sins, and to seek my own salvation with the Lord's help. God could not force me to do anything I did not want to do. I had to make the choice and the request.

I had wasted years of not being able to talk with my Father in Heaven and receive His answers. As a young Jewish girl, I had yearned for this communication with God. How much greater would have been my experience growing up if I had just known the true way to pray.

God

I asked the missionaries to describe God for me. I was told we address God as our Heavenly Father because we are His spirit children. We have "a special relationship with him that differentiates man from all other created things: man is literally God's offspring, made in his image, whereas all other things are but the work of his hands" (LDS Bible Dictionary, God, pg. 681; Acts 17:28–29). God has a body of flesh and bones and is a glorified person, tangible and perfected. He loves us. He weeps with us when we suffer and rejoices when we do what is right. He will never force us to do good. We must choose for ourselves for we are free agents and responsible for our own acts.

He wants to communicate with us when we ask, and we can communicate with Him through sincere, heartfelt prayer. I was so happy to hear this as I already knew that God was real, and it was so refreshing to find another church that believed the same thing that I knew to be right. He is the Supreme Governor of the universe and the Father of mankind.

JESUS CHRIST

I was taught a lot about Jesus Christ, the Son of God, whom I knew from the New Testament. He also had a tangible, glorified and resurrected body. He was real. He is still alive. I learned that the gospel is very simple. It includes faith in the Lord Jesus Christ, repentance of sin, baptism by immersion for the remittance of sin by someone with the proper authority, the laying on of hands for the gift of the Holy Ghost, and then keeping the commandments until the end. They explained each step of this in detail, so I could understand the importance and how it related to me.

I learned what the term resurrection and atonement meant and how it applied to me. They explained to me that we all suffer physical death, but Jesus Christ overcame this for us when He died on the cross. His spirit became separated from His body, and on the third day, His spirit and body were reunited, eternally, never to be separated again. He appeared to many people showing them that He had an immortal, tangible body of flesh and bone. The reuniting of body and spirit is called resurrection. I understood this before, but then they said, because of the Resurrection of Jesus Christ, we will all be resurrected regardless of whether we have done good or evil in this life. We will all have an immortal body of flesh and bones that will never again be subject to disease, pain or death. The resurrection makes it possible to return to God's presence to be judged but does not guarantee we will be able to live in His presence. To receive that blessing, we must also be cleansed from sin.

The missionaries also explained to me that I was made up of a spirit and a body. My spirit was ancient and lived before being born into this world and would continue living forever. I was Nancy before

I came to this earth. I am Nancy here on earth. I will be Nancy after my body dies. I learned that my mortal body may die but that my eternal spirit continues forever.

God also sent His Beloved Son, Jesus Christ, to overcome, by the Atonement, the obstacle of sin in addition to the obstacle of physical death. So we are not responsible for the sin of Adam and Eve, but are responsible for our own sins. This cleared up many of the different doctrines I heard from other churches.

I learned through the Atonement of the Savior we can become clean from sin, so that we can live with God again. But we have to do our part! We can only become clean of sin by having faith in Jesus Christ, repenting from sin with a true repentance. In other words, if we commit sin, we need to stop it, make amends if possible, and ask for forgiveness, and never repeat the sin. They explained that there is no confusion on this point. Jesus Christ knows what we do and how we think. There is no way to excuse or cover up our sins. After we repent, we can decide to be baptized by someone who has the authority of God, so that this baptism will last past death and stand forever. After baptism comes the gift of the Holy Ghost by the laying on of hands by someone with authority. Then we are to keep the commandments of God which they said they would fully explain later.

Finally, I began to understand these words—resurrection, atonement, repentance, baptism and gift of the Holy Ghost.

I wanted to know where all the information they were explaining to me came from. They told me about Joseph Smith and how revelation, inspiration, and the priesthood were restored to a modern prophet. They explained to me that many plain and precious things had been lost or omitted from the Bible, leaving us in some confusion—that after the death of all the ancient Apostles, the true gospel had been changed or lost. This time in the history of the earth was known as the "Dark Ages." They said that the knowledge that had been lost has now been restored in its fullness by revelation from Jesus Christ to a living prophet.

I thought, well, that made sense. It rang true. Now, line upon line, precept upon precept, I was beginning to understand the complete gospel. As I was being taught, I was asked to go home and pray to Heavenly Father and ask Him if what I was learning were true. That way I would know, not from man alone, but from God, through the Holy Ghost.

The Holy Ghost

The missionaries explained to me that I could know the truth when I prayed to God in faith and sincerity asking a specific question. The answer would come to me by the power of the Holy Ghost whose job is to communicate with us and tell us all truth. His primary job is to testify to us that Jesus Christ is the Son of God. I realize now it was the Holy Ghost that communicated with me at Rainbow Bridge. It was there I had been filled with the Holy Spirit and given this precious knowledge. I learned that the Holy Ghost usually communicates to us in three ways (1) feeling a marvelous sense of peace that cannot come except from God; (2) hearing a still small voice inside of our mind; (3) a burning feeling in our chest. When this occurred, I would know that it is from the Holy Ghost and not from man. I thought, if I prayed, and felt this same spiritual feeling as I did at Rainbow Bridge, I could not make a mistake.

The Holy Ghost does not have a body. He is separate from God and Jesus Christ and is a personage of spirit. God is a separate being, Jesus Christ, His Son, is also separate, and both have tangible bodies. Together with the Holy Ghost, they form what is called the Godhead. All three of them are unified with the same purpose and therefore are "one" in purpose.

I understood that all my prayers would not be answered in this way. Sometimes I would not feel the Spirit. Many times I could just talk with God and pour out my heart to Him and not really ask Him for an answer. If I asked for blessings or needs, I had to realize that many times the answer might be no. When I felt the Holy Spirit I would recognize it, and the answer I received was personal just for me or my family and not for others or the Church. Only the prophet could receive instruction and revelation for the Church.

THE PROPHET JOSEPH SMITH AND THE RESTORATION OF THE CHURCH OF JESUS CHRIST

I was told about a living Prophet Joseph Smith and how the Book of Mormon was translated by him through the power of God. The Prophet Joseph received commandments and revelations from Jesus Christ to organize His Church which is recorded in detail in the Doctrine and Covenants. This book is also one of the standard works or scriptures of The Church of Jesus Christ of Latter-day Saints. I read with interest these words:

> And gave him [Joseph Smith] power from on high, by the means which were before prepared [Urim and Thummim], to translate the Book of Mormon;
>
> Which contains a record of a fallen people, and the fullness of the gospel of Jesus Christ to the Gentiles and to the Jews also;
>
> Which was given by inspiration and is confirmed to others by the ministering of angels, and is declared unto the world by them—
>
> Proving to the world that the holy scriptures are true, and that God does inspire men and call them to his holy work in this age and generation, as well as in generations of old;
>
> Thereby showing that he is the same God yesterday, today and forever. Amen. [D&C 20:8–12]

I remember reading about the Urim and Thummim in the Old Testament, "And he [Moses] put the breastplate upon him [Aaron]: also he put in the breastplate the Urim and the Thummim" (Leviticus 8:8). This was part of the clothing for Aaron when he was consecrated high priest before all Israel by Moses. "And he [Moses] poured of the

anointing oil upon Aaron's head, and anointed him, to sanctify him"
(Leviticus 8:12).

I thought it was very interesting that Joseph Smith translated the
Book of Mormon using the Urim and Thummim, the same instru-
ment used in ancient times by the Jewish prophets.

So the question I had to answer for myself was whether Joseph
Smith was truly a prophet and had received the full gospel of Jesus
Christ? Did he translate the Book of Mormon by the power of God?
I know that I felt a connection to God when I read the Book of
Mormon, but I had not asked God if it were true. I wanted to learn
more before I asked God.

If what I was hearing were true, I could see the link between our
ancient religion and successive ages. God gave an ancient prophet His
gospel, who taught it to the people; later the people apostatized and
lost the true faith. Then another prophet was appointed by God who
again taught the true faith, and again this prophet was not believed
and perhaps killed. This cycle continued over and over again. I now
could see God gave His religion to Father Adam followed by apostasy,
then to Noah followed by apostasy, then to Abraham, followed by
apostasy, then to Moses, followed by apostasy, then to Jesus Christ,
followed by universal apostasy. It was finally given, for these last days,
to the Prophet Joseph Smith. "Unto whom [Joseph Smith] I have
committed the keys of my kingdom, and a dispensation of the gospel
for the last times; and for the fullness of times, in the which I will
gather together in one all things, both which are in heaven, and which
are on earth" (D&C 27:13).

The Book of Mormon described the same scenario of a prophet,
restoration, and apostasy. As I sat there thinking about these words I
realized that this was the last opportunity we have to understand the
gospel and accept it. Not just pieces of truth here and there, but all
knowledge and spiritual power we could desire or need. This is the
final and last dispensation of the gospel.

RESTORATION OF THE PRIESTHOOD
OR AUTHORITY TO ACT FOR GOD

If Joseph Smith were a prophet then everything I was learning would be true also. I decided to read the Doctrine and Covenants.

The Explanatory Introduction says:

> This is a collection of divine revelations and inspired declarations given for the establishment and regulation of the kingdom of God on the earth in the last days. The messages, warnings, and exhortations are for the benefit of all mankind, and contain an invitation to all people everywhere to hear the voice of the Lord Jesus Christ, speaking to them for their temporal well-being and their everlasting salvation. Most of the revelations in this compilation were received through Joseph Smith, Jun., the first prophet and president of The Church of Jesus Christ of Latter-day Saints. Others were issued through some of his successors in the Presidency.

I loved reading this book. It was revealed in English, did not have to be translated, and was easy to understand. My mind started to learn of things beyond this earth. I felt like a new world opened up to me and that I was learning things not only by reading but also from the Spirit. I felt what I can only describe as spiritual inspiration many times as I read the words of Jesus Christ. These words penetrated my heart. I read over and over again the first few paragraphs of this book for they had a way of reaching into my soul.

> Hearken, O ye people of my church, saith the voice of him who dwells on high, and whose eyes are upon all men; yea, verily I say: Hearken ye people from afar; and ye that are upon the islands of the sea, listen together.
> For verily the voice of the Lord is unto all men, and there is none to escape; and there is no eye that shall not see, neither ear that shall not hear, neither heart that shall not be penetrated. [D&C 1:1–2]

As I read this book, Doctrine and Covenants, it became clear to me that God does everything in an orderly way. He does not change

His doctrine from one generation to the next but is consistent, orderly, and organized in everything He does.

I found it fascinating to read the words of our Lord Jesus Christ, my Jewish Messiah, and how He reveals His will and knowledge to a living prophet in our day and in our own language. I read with great interest the words in Doctrine and Covenants where Jesus Christ revealed the authority of the priesthood which had been handed down from prophet to prophet since the beginning (but frequently rejected by the people). He said "I have committed the keys [to Joseph Smith] of bringing to pass the restoration of all things spoken by the mouth of *all* the holy prophets since the world began, concerning the last days;" (D&C 27:6, emphasis added). I realized that there was a beautiful, logical plan that included the Jews and Gentiles that started with Adam and continues to this day.

I learned that Joseph Smith was given the priesthood by angels sent by God and ordained first to the Aaronic Priesthood and then later to the higher or Melchizedek Priesthood. The Doctrine and Covenants describes these priesthoods.

AARONIC PRIESTHOOD

> The power and authority of the lesser, or Aaronic Priesthood, is to hold the keys of the ministering of angels, and to administer in outward ordinances, the letter of the gospel, the baptism of repentance for the remission of sins, agreeable to the covenants and commandments. [D&C 107:20]

This was the priesthood that was described in the Old Testament in the days of Moses. It was named after Moses' brother Aaron. Now I understood that the Aaronic Priesthood had the authority to perform the baptism of repentance for remission of sins. I thought that information answered a very big question. So John the Baptist had the authority to baptize people for remission of sin as a holder of the Aaronic Priesthood. This was possibly part of the Jewish beliefs at that time since many Jews were baptized by John *before* Jesus Christ was baptized. This must have been an ancient Jewish doctrine, and baptism was not invented by the Christians after all (see Mark 1:4).

MELCHIZEDEK PRIESTHOOD

> The power and authority of the higher, or Melchizedek Priesthood, is to hold the keys of all the spiritual blessings of the church—
>
> To have the privilege of receiving the mysteries of the kingdom of heaven, to have the heavens opened unto them, to commune with the general assembly and church of the Firstborn [Jesus Christ], and to enjoy the communion and presence of God the Father, and Jesus the mediator of the new covenant. [D&C 107:18–19]

I read the next scriptures over and over because this was a totally new idea to me. Moses had the Melchizedek Priesthood given to him by Jethro, his father-in-law (see D&C 84:6). The next succeeding verses trace the authority of the priesthood from Jethro back through his ancestors, then ultimately to Abraham, Noah, Enoch, Abel, and then Adam.

> Which priesthood continueth in the church of God in all generations, and is without beginning of days or end of years . . . .
>
> And this greater [Melchizedek] priesthood administereth the gospel and holdeth the key of the mysteries of the kingdom, even the key of the knowledge of God.
>
> Therefore, in the ordinances thereof, the power of godliness is manifest.
>
> And without the ordinances thereof, and the authority of the priesthood, the power of godliness is not manifest unto men in the flesh. [D&C 84:17, 19–21]

But then why did the tribes of Israel only have the Aaronic Priesthood and not the Melchizedek? The modern scriptures continue:

> Now this Moses plainly taught to the children of Israel in the wilderness, and sought diligently to sanctify his people that they might behold the face of God; [which means that they might receive the higher or Melchizedek Priesthood].

But they hardened their hearts and could not endure his presence; therefore, the Lord in his wrath, for his anger was kindled against them, swore that they should not enter into his rest while in the wilderness, which rest is the fullness of his glory.

Therefore, *he took Moses out of their midst, and the Holy Priesthood also;*

And the lesser priesthood continued, which priesthood holdeth the key of the ministering of angels and the preparatory gospel;

Which gospel is the gospel of repentance and of baptism, and the remission of sins, and the law of carnal commandments, which the Lord in his wrath caused to continue with the house of Aaron among the children of Israel until John, whom God raised up . . . .

. . . to make straight the way of the Lord before the face of his people, to prepare them for the coming of the Lord, in whose hand is given all power. [D&C 84:23–28, emphasis added]

What wonderful new knowledge. It answers fully so many questions. I also learned that all worthy men in the Church can be ordained first to the Aaronic Priesthood and later to the Melchizedek Priesthood. These ordinances must be performed by one who holds the Holy Melchizedek Priesthood. Priesthood is not dependent upon lineage. This is a great responsibility. The authority, duties, and organization for these priesthoods is spelled out in various sections of the Doctrine and Covenants. A man must live a righteous life to hold the holy priesthood and exercise its powers.

So here were additional links from ancient Judaism to the fullness of the gospel. I was thrilled to learn this new information:

- A true, living, and personal God who was real and still provided miracles on the earth.
- That Jesus Christ was the Messiah, the Son of God, the Savior and Redeemer of the whole world including the Jews.
- A living prophet to receive revelation from God for the people.
- The restoration of the ancient Aaronic Priesthood and then the higher Melchizedek Priesthood authority.

- The Book of Mormon, Doctrine and Covenants, and Pearl of Great Price, three books that are Latter-day Saint scriptures that have been received through the power of God.
- The Book of Mormon was translated using the Urim and Thummim, just as it was used by the ancient prophets.
- Baptism was part of the functions of the Aaronic Priesthood and carnal commandments.
- The power of prayer and that prayers can be answered.

JOSEPH SMITH TRANSLATION OF THE BIBLE

After reading in Doctrine and Covenants about the Melchizedek Priesthood being taken from the Israelites, I wanted to understand what happened at Mt. Sinai. In Exodus, I read about two sets of tablets that Moses obtained. So what was on the first set? I thought both sets were the same. I now learned the true meaning of the famous scripture in the Old Testament Exodus 34:1–2.

The Prophet Joseph Smith was commanded by the Lord to correct some of the errors in the Bible. He started this work in the year 1830 and did not complete it before his death. Extracts from his manuscript now appear in the Latter-day Saint edition of the Bible as footnotes with lengthy quotes in the Appendix. Longer portions such as Genesis chapters 1–8 appear as the book of Moses in the Pearl of Great Price.

I have copied below Exodus 34:1–2. **The words in italics are the ones that were omitted or removed from the original Bible version, but restored by Joseph Smith the Prophet through the inspiration of the Lord:**

> And the Lord said unto Moses, Hew thee two *other* tables of stone, like unto the first, and I will write upon *them also,* the words of *the law, according as they were written at the first on the* tables which thou brakest; *but it shall not be according to the first, for I will take away the priesthood out of their midst; therefore my holy order, and the ordinances*

thereof, shall not go before them; for my presence shall not go up in their midst, lest I destroy them.

But I will give unto them the law as at the first, but it shall be after the law of a carnal commandment; for I have sworn in my wrath, that they shall not enter into my presence, into my rest, in the days of their pilgrimage. Therefore do as I have commanded thee, and be ready in the morning, and come up in the morning unto mount Sinai. [Exodus 34:1–2, Joseph Smith Translation, page 800 Latter-day Saint edition of the Bible]

I understood for the first time the consequences of worshiping the golden calf. That is, Israel was left with only the lesser or Aaronic Priesthood! They were left with only half of the gospel. How different the twelve tribes of Israel would have been if they had the fullness of the higher or Melchizedek Priesthood. For the first time, I realized the treasure of the new information now before me.

It was much later, after I joined the Church, that I started to understand the power of the Melchizedek Priesthood to do good, as it is given to righteous men on the earth. The loss of this priesthood in ancient times made me weep. But the restoration of the priesthood now fills my heart with joy to think that some day that righteous Jewish men will receive this ancient priesthood that they lost at Mt. Sinai. While the lesser priesthood was given only to the members of the Tribe of Levi; now the Melchizedek Priesthood can be received by any worthy man of any tribe or nation.

We had the temple built by Moses in accordance with the Aaronic Priesthood authority. If the Melchizedek Priesthood had been accepted by the Israelites at Mt. Sinai, then also the temple ordinances that corresponded to that priesthood would have also been operational.

PRIESTHOOD BLESSINGS

I was taught that the righteous men of The Church of Jesus Christ of Latter-day Saints who hold the Melchizedek priesthood had the authority to lay hands on my head and give me a blessing from

God. This blessing could be for the healing of the sick or a blessing for something that was concerning me, and I needed spiritual guidance. It was predicated upon my faith. It made sense to me to be able to depend on the power of God through His priesthood to receive blessings from Him. The idea of a spiritual guide as described in the psychic world was a very poor substitute for the truth and reality of God's blessings.

I was told of many instances, recorded in The Church of Jesus Christ of Latter-day Saint history, of the healing of the sick, the blind that could see, and even people that were brought back to life. They explained that the true Church of Jesus Christ must have in it all the spiritual gifts that were available at the time Jesus Christ and His Apostles were on the earth.

TEMPLES ANCIENT AND MODERN

I was taught about special places that have been built by the Church that are called temples. Temples were known to me from my Jewish upbringing. I knew about the first temple (tabernacle) built by Moses in the wilderness. Then there was Solomon's temple built under the guidance of God.

I learned that modern temples had also been built at the command of God. They have been built by the Church and are now in use. Just as Moses was commanded to build a temple, so was the Prophet Joseph Smith.

Before I could understand the need for a temple, I had to know about the eternal plan of God for us. I was given instruction on: (1) The premortal world where all of us started as spirit children; (2) Our mortal world where we get bodies and learn by experience; (3) What happens after we die when our spirit separates from our body and goes to the spirit world; (4) Judgment by Jesus Christ for our actions on the earth and assignment to either the telestial, terrestrial, or celestial kingdoms according to personal righteousness or wickedness;

(5) Resurrection when the body and spirit are united forever.

I was then told about the doctrine of eternal families. This was the greatest doctrine of all for me. It pulled together all the other information that I had learned and allowed me a glimpse into a future that only God and His Son Jesus Christ could provide for us if we are faithful and kept the commandments. In order for us to have an eternal family in heaven, the ancient power of Elijah and his priesthood to seal on earth and in heaven had to be restored (see 1 Kings 17:1, Malachi 4:5–6). It was restored to the Prophet Joseph Smith in 1836.

I was asked to read Doctrine and Covenants 110:13–16 with regard to Elijah. This was of great interest, because I never understood who Elijah was and why we always set a place for him at our Passover table. I read the following: In Kirtland, Ohio, April 3, 1836 visions were manifested to Joseph Smith the Prophet and Oliver Cowdery:

> . . . another great and glorious vision burst upon us; for Elijah the prophet, who was taken to heaven without tasting death, stood before us, and said:
>
> Behold, the time has fully come, which was spoken of by the mouth of Malachi—testifying that he [Elijah] should be sent, before the great and dreadful day of the Lord come—
>
> To turn the hearts of the fathers to the children, and the children to the fathers, lest the whole earth be smitten with a curse—
>
> Therefore, the keys of this dispensation are committed into your hands; and by this ye may know that the great and dreadful day of the Lord is near, even at the doors. [D&C 110:13–16]

I rejoiced when I read this doctrine about children on earth and fathers in the spirit world turning their hearts to each other. There was a reason why the prophet Elijah was remembered at Passover; and now I understood his purpose. Passover is a family event when families gather together. This ancient celebration has occurred over centuries as each family continued this tradition. How appropriate that Elijah, whose power to bind and seal families together should be remembered at that time. Elijah's promised coming is now fulfilled, and we no longer need to expect him at Passover.

What marvelous words and what a great feeling I had. The sealing power that was restored by the prophet Elijah would be given by the prophet to special Melchizedek Priesthood holders in the Church to be used in the temple to seal, or marry, families together forever, for time and all eternity.

I realized as I pondered this information that this was the fulfillment of God's covenant with Abraham. His posterity would be as numerous as the stars of heaven. This promise could only be fulfilled if his marriage continued, not just in this world but forever. Our Father in Heaven had given His faithful children the greatest gift of all, the ability to have our marriages and our families with us for all eternity even after death. I felt heaven could never be heaven without my loved ones and my family with me. Who wants to live isolated and alone forever as a single person?

So now I could add other links:

- The coming of Elijah the Prophet (see Malachi 4:5–6)
- The covenant of Abraham having a way to be fulfilled

KEEPING THE COMMANDMENTS

I was taught that, as members of the Church, we must keep the commandments of God. The main commandments are mostly from the Ten Commandments (see Exodus 20). These are the permanent laws of God. How refreshing to hear this in a day where sin is acceptable and commonplace. The members of this Church have standards and they are expected to live by them. In fact, in some instances when they are broken and not repented of Church discipline follows. The commandments are:

- Keep the Sabbath day holy.

- Thou shalt not commit adultery "nor do anything like unto it" (D&C 59:6).
- The law of chastity. This is of utmost importance to the Lord. This means no pre-marital sex. Also fidelity to your spouse after marriage.
- The law of obedience to the commandments of God as revealed through prophets. This is an ancient law.
- The law of tithing. This is also an ancient law as when Abraham paid tithes to Melchizedek (seeGenesis 14:20, Malachi 3:8).
- The Word of Wisdom. In 1833 the Lord revealed the Word of Wisdom to Joseph Smith. This law asks us to not smoke, drink alcohol, drink coffee or tea or take drugs. It is amazing to think that the Lord was warning us against these vices so long ago. To comply with this, all I had to give up was a one-half cup of coffee each morning.
- Fasting and prayer.
- No lying, stealing, or killing.

I was thrilled to hear this. These were God's laws. I lived by them already and was so pleased to hear that these were the standards of the members of the Church. In fact I learned that I had to make a commitment to live by these laws before joining the Church. This was true of all the members. This was not a social club I would be joining, but The Church of Jesus Christ of Latter-day Saints. If I wanted to feel the Holy Spirit and receive inspiration I had to follow the Lord's commandments. I also was informed that not all members were perfect and that repentance is an ongoing law. But it was up to us to do our absolute best to follow all of God's laws.

I was taught the Ten Commandments as a Jewish child and learned to live by them. It pleased me that the members of this church were asked to do the same.

ATTENDING CHURCH

Debra and Mike were the members who invited me to their home for the missionary lessons. They explained to me how the gospel blessed their lives. They were kind and became dear friends. They invited me to attend church with them. They explained that the Church was divided up into wards—each one contained approximately 300 members. A bishop and two counselors were in charge of the ward. Groups of wards totaling approximately 2000 members were called a stake, with a stake president and two counselors who were in charge of this larger group. They explained that neither the bishops, his counselors, the stake president nor his counselors, nor any workers in the ward or stakes are paid. Everyone has their own employment outside of the Church to earn his or her own living. This fact thrilled me as I thought of the greed in the world.

I will never forget my first Church meeting. I walked into church and was greeted by many people whom I had never met. I felt welcome. I sat with Mike and Debra. They had previously explained to me that church was three hours long. The first hour was the sacrament meeting where righteous members partook of the sacrament. During sacrament meeting, we also sang hymns and two or three members were asked to give talks about a gospel subject. I remember so clearly a teenage girl got up to speak. Her topic was spiritual battles. I was very alert when I heard her subject. She related a story to us. She had been invited to a beach party, and her parents did not want her to go. They said it was dangerous, and there would probably be drinking. She said she wanted to go and disobeyed her parents. She said she knew, from the teachings of the Church, and from the Spirit that she should not go. She went anyway. She said it was like the cartoons, God on her right shoulder, telling her "not to go" and Satan, on her left shoulder, saying, "nothing will happen. You should be allowed to make your own decisions." She said the party lasted a long time and many were drinking alcohol. To get home, the only transportation was in the back of a pickup truck. She piled in with the other teenagers but was afraid as the driver had been drinking. They had a bad accident, and she lost her eyesight. Some of her friends were killed. She said she had received a priesthood blessing in the hospital and was promised that her sight would return. She testified that her sight did return and that it was a miracle. She will never forget the lesson of always obeying the commandments of god and listening to the Spirit. I was amazed at her words. What insight she had.

After the sacrament meeting, we went to either Sunday School to study the scriptures or the Gospel Principles class for investigators like me. The Sunday School teaches in succeeding years the Old Testament, New Testament, Book of Mormon, Doctrine and Covenants and Pearl of Great Price and the History of the Church. I decided to go to Sunday School with Mike and Debra.

The third hour, we split up into two groups. The women went to ward Relief Society which, in the whole Church, is the oldest and largest women's organization in the world. We were taught how to apply gospel principles in our everyday lives. The men went to priesthood meetings.

Debra told me that the teachings of the Church were the same in every one of the 28,000 wards in the world. I could go to Dallas, Texas or Sydney, Australia or Brazil or the Philippines and the same lessons would be taught at the same time everywhere. There was one gospel and one faith taught. The books and lessons were prepared under the direction of our prophet and apostles called the First Presidency and the Quorum of the Twelve. This answered my question about one true church.

I enjoyed my time in church and was faithful in going every Sunday when I was able. Debra explained to me that on the first Sunday of every month, the members were asked to fast by skipping two meals. The money saved from not eating these two meals would be given to the bishop as fast offerings to be used for the poor and needy. Also, on fast day, during sacrament meeting, instead of talks, the members could get up and bear their testimonies of the truth of the gospel and how God had blessed their lives. I remember the first time I went to fast and testimony meeting. My heart was truly touched.

PROCRASTINATING

I was taught all the lessons of the basic doctrine of the Church. So the missionaries asked me if I wanted to be baptized? I thought I had already been baptized by God at Rainbow Bridge, so I did not think it was necessary for me. The missionaries explained again to me the necessity to be baptized by authority into The Church of Jesus Christ of Latter-day Saints.

I was enjoying learning and studying and attending church meetings. But joining the Church as a member was something that I had to think about. I knew that if I joined, I would be committed to all the teachings of the Church. How would my life change? Would it be better or worse? Fear and doubt continually coursed through my mind. I now realize that fear and doubt are tools of Satan. He wanted to stop me from progressing spiritually. People heard about my investigating this church and gave me anti-Mormon books to read. But I did not read them. I did not want to be diverted. I kept my focus on studying the gospel and learning more and more.

I was encouraged by the missionaries who were teaching me to ask God, in prayer, if the Book of Mormon were true. I read, over and over, a promise in the Introduction of the Book of Mormon that says, "We invite all men everywhere to read the Book of Mormon, to ponder in their hearts the message it contains, and then to ask God, the Eternal Father, in the name of Christ if the book is true. Those who pursue this course and ask in faith will gain a testimony of its truth and divinity by the power of the Holy Ghost" (see also Moroni 10:3–5). But I did not ask.

I continued to read the Book of Mormon to gain a better understanding of Jesus Christ. I was astonished to find these words:

But thus saith the Lord God: O fools, they shall have a Bible; and it shall proceed forth from the Jews, mine ancient covenant people. And what thank they the Jews for the Bible which they receive from them? Yea, what do the Gentiles mean? Do they remember the travails and the labors and the pains of the Jews, and their diligence unto me, in bringing forth salvation unto the Gentiles?

O ye Gentiles, have ye remembered the Jews, mine ancient covenant people? Nay; but ye have cursed them and have hated them, and have not sought to recover them. But behold, I will return all these things upon your own heads; for I the Lord have not forgotten my people. [2 Nephi 29:4–5]

I was happy to hear these words in the Book of Mormon thanking the Jews for their contribution. I had not heard this doctrine taught anywhere else. It was truly refreshing, and I felt good about it.

I was learning line upon line, precept upon precept the big picture of the gospel with all its glorious links to ancient Judaism. I thought I could just go on learning and studying. Did I really need to make a decision to be baptized and join the Church? Baptism for a Jewish girl into this church was a big step.

CHAPTER 4

A Member of the Church of Jesus Christ of Latter-day Saints

(1996)

> Now when they heard this, they were pricked in their heart, and said unto Peter and to the rest of the apostles, Men and brethren, what shall we do?
>
> Then Peter said unto them, Repent, and be baptized every one of you in the name of Jesus Christ for the remission of sins, and ye shall receive the gift of the Holy Ghost.
>
> For the promise is unto you, and to your children, and to all that are afar off, even as many as the Lord our God shall call. [Acts 2:37–39]
>
> Wherefore teach it unto your children, that all men, everywhere, must repent, or they can in nowise inherit the kingdom of God, for no unclean thing can dwell there, or dwell in his presence; for, in the language of Adam, Man of Holiness is his name, and the name of his Only Begotten is the Son of Man, even Jesus Christ, a righteous Judge, who shall come in the meridian of time.
>
> Therefore I give unto you a commandment, to teach these things freely unto your children, saying:
>
> That by reason of transgression cometh the fall, which fall bringeth death, and inasmuch as ye were born into the world by water, and blood, and the spirit, which I have made, and so became of dust a living soul, even so ye must be born again into the kingdom of heaven, of water, and of the Spirit, and be cleansed by blood, even the blood of mine Only Begotten; that ye might be sanctified from all sin, and enjoy the words of eternal life in this world, and eternal life in the world to come, even immortal glory. [Moses 6:57–59]

My Faith is Growing

One of my friends, who had been investigating the Church with me, decided to be baptized. When she was confirmed a member of The Church of Jesus Christ of Latter-day Saints and received the gift of the Holy Ghost, I saw a new light come into her eyes.

I still had some questions about being baptized myself. I read over and over in the scriptures of the need for baptism as a gate to enter into the kingdom of heaven. But what did this really mean? What would I feel like if I decided to be baptized into The Church of Jesus Christ of Latter-day Saints? How could I feel any better than I did at Rainbow Bridge? Would I stop being Jewish? I would need a confirmation from God to do this. What would it feel like to have the gift of the Holy Ghost? I already felt the Holy Ghost once in awhile; why would this be different?

When I read that Jesus Christ was baptized by John the Baptist, a question arose in my mind. Why did Jesus Christ go to John the Baptist, who was of the pure blood of Aaron and a holder of the Aaronic Priesthood, to be baptized? Was baptism an accepted Jewish practice by the Aaronic Priesthood in ancient times, and did John have the authority to baptize? As I said before, I learned from the teachings of the Church that the Priesthood of Aaron, "holds the keys of the ministering of angels, and of the gospel of repentance and of *baptism by immersion for the remission of sins*" (D&C 13:1, emphasis added).

Jesus Christ Himself was baptized even though He had no sins at all, but He said: "Suffer it to be so now: for thus it becometh us to fulfill all righteousness" (Matthew 3:15). In the Book of Mormon it says:

> And now, if the Lamb of God, he being holy, should have need to be baptized by water, to fulfil all righteousness, O then, how much more need have we, being unholy, to be baptized, yea, even by water!
>
> . . . notwithstanding he being holy, he showeth unto the children of men that, according to the flesh he humbleth himself before the

Father, and witnesseth unto the Father that he would be obedient unto him in keeping his commandments.

Wherefore, after he was baptized with water the Holy Ghost descended upon him in the form of a dove.

And again, it showeth unto the children of men the straitness of the path, and the narrowness of the gate, by which they should enter, he having set the example before them. [2 Nephi 31:5, 7–9]

My conclusion was that baptism was required of every accountable person to get into the kingdom of God and had to be done by someone with the priesthood authority given to him from God.

Why would the Christian churches through the centuries force a false baptism on my ancestors or else die? From what I learned about baptism from The Church of Jesus Christ of Latter-day Saints, to partake of this ordinance requires personal choice after repentance and a change of heart. A forced baptism is of no value. It also requires us after baptism to "willingly take upon us the name of Jesus Christ, having a determination to serve Him to the end, and truly manifest by their works that they have received of the Spirit of Christ unto the remission of their sins" (D&C 20:37).

Was I ready to make this commitment? I was getting closer to saying yes. I was thinking about all of this when my friend took the step and was baptized into the Church.

Our friends, Debra and Mike, had a party in their home for my friend after her baptism. Debra said to me when I approached her, "You have been disobedient of God. Who are you to not to be baptized when Jesus Christ was baptized? You must take care of yourself first!" She later told me that the Spirit of the Lord asked her to say those words to me in a stern tone of voice. She did not want to say these words to me but the Spirit was insistent.

When I heard her words, I was cut to the core of my being. I did not want to be disobedient of God. I thought I was obeying God. I thought I had been baptized at Rainbow Bridge, but here she was saying to me that I needed to be baptized into His true Church. It was because of these words and the way they were said that I went home and knew that it was time for me to ask God for an answer.

God Revealed the Truth to Me

When I arrived home, I immediately got on my knees and with tears in my eyes asked God for forgiveness. I did not want to be disobedient. I wanted the truth, and I was ready to receive an answer. I cried and cried for what seemed to me like hours, and talked to God in a way that I had never done before. This time I was asking the right questions and seeking answers. I now knew how to communicate with God through personal, heartfelt prayer.

I said, "Dear Heavenly Father, I thank Thee for the words I heard tonight and ask Thee for forgiveness. I thought I was being obedient. I want the truth about this Church! I am ready to hear the truth from Thee. There is a promise in the Book of Mormon that if I ask in faith, I will receive an answer by the Holy Ghost. I want an answer to my questions." So I asked, "Should I be baptized into the Church of Jesus Christ of Latter-day Saints? Is the Book of Mormon true? Is Joseph Smith a prophet of God? Are the teachings that I have learned from this Church true?" I asked many other questions. I ended my prayer in the name of Jesus Christ, amen."

After my prayer, I waited for an answer. I was exhausted and still had no answer, so I went to sleep.

I was awakened at 3:00 o'clock in the morning by the Holy Spirit. I felt a powerful spiritual presence and connection to God. I realized that what I felt was the Holy Ghost. I heard a quiet voice inside of my mind say that I was to be baptized immediately into The Church of Jesus Christ of Latter-day Saints. The Book of Mormon was true and Joseph Smith was a prophet of God.

I asked more questions and received answers. I was so happy. I knew that I was on the right course this time. I knew the answer did not come from anyone on this earth, but from my Father in Heaven.

My Baptism

Four days later, on May 30, 1996, I was baptized into The Church of Jesus Christ of Latter-day Saints. I was also confirmed a member of the Church and, by the laying on of hands by a Melchizedek Priesthood holder with authority, I received the gift of the Holy Ghost. I remember the words that coursed through my mind at that moment. *I am home.* I knew that this was true. I felt so clean and pure that my sins were forgiven. What a great blessing repentance followed by a cleansing baptism were in my life. I put my old life behind me and started a new life from that moment on. I was determined to keep the commandments of God and serve the Lord Jesus Christ.

I learned the process of baptism is of great importance. We are commanded by our Lord Jesus Christ to repent and be baptized. This is a true doctrine and not one to be taken lightly. I knew that when I was baptized by someone with the true authority of God that I would be clean, sweet, and pure and that my baptism would be valid in heaven. I would be forgiven of my sins through the Atonement of Jesus Christ, if I had repented of them. Repentance is not done in a day or a moment, but is a process of forsaking our sins and seeking forgiveness from our Lord through His Atonement. It requires our faith in the Lord Jesus Christ. I was ashamed of myself for waiting so long to be baptized into this Church and receive these blessings.

My life before my baptism was not without blemish, but I now had a new chance to start fresh and be forgiven of all my sins. What a great and everlasting blessing. My heart and mind had to be right before the Lord for He knew me so well. He could read my thoughts and the intents of my heart. If I were to partake of the cleansing power of our Lord, through baptism, then I had to be completely truthful about my life. I wanted this with all my heart.

I would not only learn the gospel but live it also. I would experience how God works in my everyday life.

I have tried my best to follow His example in all that I do. Because of this, I am happy and no longer bothered by my past sins. If I ignore the commandments of God, I make a mockery of this ordinance. Thus, to be baptized means that we must be of an age that we can repent first. Otherwise, what is the purpose of baptism?

It is now almost ten years later, and I can now look back on that moment in time when I was baptized. Because I have tried to keep the commandments of God and have tried with great effort to serve the Lord Jesus Christ, my life has changed for the good. I can see such a difference in the person that I am now and the person that I used to be. I like who I am. I am grateful for my baptism, the gift of the Holy Ghost that I depend on everyday, and the power of the restored priesthood that enabled me to partake of these glorious ordinances of the gospel of Jesus Christ in their fullness. It amazes me now that I procrastinated so long before being baptized and joining The Church of Jesus Christ of Latter-day Saints.

God and Jesus Christ
Became More Personal to Me

After baptism, my life changed for the better. I was happy, clean, and sweet like a new born baby.

God was no longer an entity whom I could not understand but was actually my Father in Heaven, who would listen to me as a father would on the earth but with much greater wisdom, power, and understanding. I had personally felt His love. Jesus Christ became very real and personal to me. I understood about the Resurrection of Jesus Christ and His Atonement for me. I was taught the meaning and truth of these events and the need for His sacrifice for me to achieve immortality and eternal life.

I, a Jewish girl, have traveled a long road to where I am now, a member of The Church of Jesus Christ of Latter-day Saints. My knowledge of spiritual matters grows everyday. There is no end to my learning, once I understood the foundation of the gospel. There is no guess work, for much has been written by modern prophets and apostles. I can receive a confirmation of the truth of all things from the Holy Ghost. This is the way spiritual learning comes to me.

I knew, with complete assurance, that Joseph Smith was a prophet of God and that the Book of Mormon was true. Therefore, I had confidence that I could study and use the information provided by both the ancient prophets of the Old and New Testaments and the Book of Mormon and the teachings of modern-day prophets of The Church of Jesus Christ of Latter-day Saints. I also learned the gospel by attending church and from the vast knowledge of our members.

THE GIFT OF THE HOLY GHOST

The gift of the Holy Ghost is a real gift. As long as I keep the commandments, stay faithful in the Church, pray, and read my scriptures I can have the companionship of the Holy Ghost. I can feel the increased strength of His peaceful influence and knowledge course into my mind as I study the gospel and live my life. I can feel His presence in times of need and directions in times of danger. I depend on His willingness to help me as I pray and ask my Father in Heaven to help or guide me.

Even now, I can feel the promptings and sometimes disregard them only to find out later that I should have heeded the feelings that I had. There is nothing too small for His attention. I remember one time I was working on a deadline, and I had an impression that my printer would run out of paper. I ignored the warning, and sure enough I ran out of paper. But this time, the machine jammed and it took me longer to fix it than only putting in new paper. I should have acted on the first inspiration.

MY FIRST CHURCH CALLING

Three months after joining the Church my bishop and his counselor came to my home. They said, "The Lord Jesus Christ wants to extend a calling to you to be a stake missionary and also to teach the Gospel Principles class on Sunday." I learned how callings were made in the Church. Our bishop and his counselors prayed about the jobs that needed to be done in the ward and received revelation from Jesus Christ who should fill these positions. That is how my bishop received his own calling. I knew my callings came from the Lord also, so I accepted. The problem was, learning what these jobs entailed. I was also set apart and given a blessing, by the laying on of hands by the bishop and his counselor before I started this church calling. I would need help from the Lord to accomplish this job. All Church callings are done this way.

As a stake missionary I was required to learn the missionary discussions and help the missionaries teach and also meet with the new members of the Church. Teaching the Gospel Principles class in Sunday School required me to learn the basic doctrine of the Church quickly. I was scheduled to teach it once a month to new members and investigators. This was a struggle for me as I was a new member. How could I possibly teach this class? Of course, these callings were wisdom in our Heavenly Father because this forced me to gain a better understanding of the gospel. I read the lesson from the *Gospel Principles* book, read all the related scriptural references from the Old and New Testaments, the Book of Mormon, the Doctrine and Covenants and other Church literature. I prayed fervently for help and received new understanding as I taught these lessons. My teaching efforts were well received. I was happy giving service to others.

The reaction to my joining the Church, by members, was most interesting. They were all wondering how a Jewish girl could join the Church of Jesus Christ. They also kept asking me questions about Judaism. I must admit that many times I had to do research on my own religion to find out the answers.

One of the classes that I was asked to teach was on the gathering of Israel. I learned in detail about the twelve tribes of Israel, their inheritance, and the prophesy of the latter-day gathering of them together again.

And I will remember the covenant which I made with my people; and I have covenanted with them that I would gather them together in mine own due time, that I would give unto them again the land of their fathers for their inheritance, which is the land of Jerusalem, which is the promised land unto them forever, saith the Father.

And it shall come to pass that the time cometh, when the fullness of my gospel shall be preached unto them;

And they shall believe in me, that I am Jesus Christ, the Son of God, and shall pray unto the Father in my name. . . .

Then will the Father, gather them together again, and give unto them Jerusalem for the land of their inheritance.

Then shall they break forth into joy—sing together, ye waste places of Jerusalem; for the Father hath comforted his people, he hath redeemed Jerusalem. [3 Nephi 20:29–31, 33-34 and Isaiah 54:1]

I sat at my desk pondering these words and thinking of Jerusalem now a nation with millions of Jewish people gathered from across the earth. Would they some day understand what I now knew that our best protection is to find faith once again in a personal, living God and His Messiah, the Lord Jesus Christ. I understood the need for this faith to protect our nation, said not in rote prayers but a personal plea to our Father in Heaven, in the name of Jesus Christ for help. These heart felt pleas must be accompanied by repentance from sin and following righteousness.

I know that our Father in Heaven is aware of His ancient covenant people. Maybe that is why I am writing this book now for I can see that events are spiraling away from us, and we will need faith, direction, comfort, and peace from a living God. I think that all of us will need miracles of God to help us in the latter days as well as the guidance of our modern prophet.

LOST BOOKS OF THE BIBLE

I continued in my quest to understand the fullness of the gospel of Jesus Christ and how it built upon the foundation of ancient

Judaism with the Old and New Testaments working together, one flowing into the other. I now had the Book of Mormon, the Doctrine and Covenants and the Pearl of Great Price to help me. But I also had a Bible Dictionary that was located at the back of the Holy Bible, Latter-day Saint edition. I looked up the section on lost books. I noticed the Old Testament referred to other books that are not now included. I assume many were lost or intentionally omitted when the Bible was compiled.

The Bible Dictionary listed the titles of books referred to in the Bible as being scripture that are not now included such as:
- Book of the Wars of the Lord (Num. 21:14)
- Book of Jasher (Josh. 10:13, Sam. 1:18)
- Book of the Acts of Solomon (1 Kgs. 11:41)
- Book of Samuel the Seer (1 Chr. 29:29)
- Book of Nathan the Prophet (1 Chr. 29:29, 2 Chr. 9:29)
- The Prophecy of Ahijah (2 Chr. 9:29)
- The Visions of Iddo the Seer (2 Chr. 9:29)
- And many others

I wonder how many of these books would have contained a reference to the Messiah, Jesus Christ?

I read in the Book of Mormon these words about Moses and Abraham:

> But, behold, ye not only deny my words, but ye also deny all the words, which have been spoken by our fathers, and also the words which were spoken by this man, Moses, who had such great power given unto him, yea, the words which he hath spoken concerning the coming of the Messiah.
>
> Yea, did he not bear record that the Son of God should come? And as he lifted up the brazen serpent in the wilderness, even so shall he be lifted up who should come.
>
> And as many as should look upon that serpent should live, even

so as many as should look upon the Son of God with faith, having a contrite spirit, might live, even unto that life which is eternal.

And now behold, Moses did not only testify of these things, but also all the holy prophets, from his days even to the days of Abraham.

Yea, and behold, Abraham saw of his coming and was filled with gladness and did rejoice . . .

Abraham not only knew of these things, but there were many before the days of Abraham who were called by the order of God; yea, even after the order of his Son; and this that it should be shown unto the people, a great many thousand years before his coming, that even redemption should come unto them. [Helaman 8:13–18]

Then the Book of Mormon text continues talking about the prophet Zenos who testified boldly of the Messiah and also Zenock, and Ezias. Isaiah and Jeremiah who also testified of the destruction of Jerusalem (see Helaman 8:19–20). Who were the prophets Zenos and Zenock? Are they part of the lost books?

So many plain and precious scriptures have been lost, but some have been restored in the Book of Mormon. I also knew that God, if He wanted to, could continue to communicate with us so maybe some of these lost books would be restored to us to provide needed information and truth.

LOST SCRIPTURES RESTORED

Months passed and I continued to learn more and more about God's revealed truth. Actually it was not like learning something new. I would describe it as remembering something that I already knew. I think this was because I learned it all in the premortal world before coming to this earth, so when I heard it, I knew it, and it rang true.

I read other scriptures restored by God to Joseph Smith entitled, the book of Moses, parts of which were omitted from the book of Genesis. This book and the book of Abraham are included in the book, Pearl of Great Price. The book of Moses, I discovered, includes what happened when Moses met God face-to-face on an exceedingly high mountain (see Moses 1:1). It described in more detail the creation of the earth, Adam and Eve, and mankind (see Moses 2–5). The importance of keeping genealogy records which was started by Adam as he recorded the information in his book of remembrance (see Moses 6:5). Information on Enoch, Noah, and the gospel of Jesus Christ that was preached from the beginning even unto Adam (see Moses 6–8). The book of Abraham was translated from an ancient record found in the catacombs of Egypt upon papyrus. This book talks about the patriarchal order, the eternal nature of spirits, and the creation of our world. "And there stood one among them that was like unto God, [Jesus Christ], and he said unto those who were with him: We will go down, for there is space there, and we will take of these materials, and we will make an earth whereon these may dwell; And we will prove them herewith, to see if they will do all things whatsoever the Lord their God shall command them" (Abraham 3:24).

I read these words in the book of Abraham. I italicized the words that had been added by modern revelation from the Lord showing the original true meaning:

> And the *Gods* formed man from the dust of the ground, *and took his spirit (that is, the man's spirit), and put it into him;* and breathed into his nostrils the breath of life, and man became a living soul [Abraham 5:7; Genesis 2:7, emphasis added]

These new words confirmed that our spirits were in existence before we came to earth.

I treasured every bit of this wonderful new information. If these books had been included in the Old Testament there would have been no doubt that Jesus Christ was our Messiah. This knowledge was taken from us and hidden for so long. I shed tears for us as a Jewish nation not understanding the plain and simple truths of our heritage. Everything is explained so simply and beautifully in these sacred books we have received from the Lord. We could not have failed to understand. But now we have many of them that have been restored to us by revelation. I know that some day all of us will know that Jesus Christ is the Messiah. These books provided a significant link between the Old and New Testaments and modern times.

GOD LIVES AND CONTINUES TO COMMUNICATE

When I discussed the idea of lost scriptures with my Christian friends, they told me that nothing new could be added to the Bible; but I knew that God continues to communicate.

Nephi, in the Book of Mormon, tells us God can speak to other nations:

> Wherefore murmur ye, because that ye shall receive more of my word? Know ye not that the testimony of two nations is a witness unto you that I am God, that I remember one nation like unto another? Wherefore I speak the same words unto one nation like unto another. And when the two nations shall run together the testimony of the two nations shall run together also.
>
> And I do this that I may prove unto many that I am the same yesterday, today, and forever; and that I speak forth my words according to mine own pleasure. And because that I have spoken one word ye need not suppose that I cannot speak another; for my work is not yet finished; neither shall it be until the end of man, neither from that time henceforth and forever. [2 Nephi 29:8–9]

Nephi continues,

> For behold, I shall speak unto the Jews and they shall write it [Bible, Stick of Judah]; and I shall also speak unto the Nephites and they shall write it [Book of Mormon, Stick of Ephraim]; and I shall also speak unto the other tribes of the house of Israel, which I have led away, and they shall write it; and I shall also speak unto all nations of the earth and they shall write it. [2 Nephi 29:12]

To me these words in the Book of Mormon are in fulfillment of the words of the prophet Ezekiel,

The word of the Lord came again unto me, saying. Moreover, thou son of man, take thee one stick and write upon it, for Judah, and for the children of Israel, his companions, then take another stick and write upon it, For Joseph, the stick of Ephraim, and for all the house of Israel his companions: And join them one to another into one stick; and they shall become one in thine hand. [Ezekiel 37:15–17]

PROPHETS AND APOSTLES

I did not truly understand the need for a living prophet until I learned what one does. A prophet receives revelation, knowledge and inspiration from the Lord, Jesus Christ, as directed by our Heavenly Father, and then he teaches it to us here on the earth. In the times of the ancient Jews, we had many prophets. From what I read in the Old Testament, we were not very diligent in following their advice nor believing in them. In ancient times, we rejected their teachings when they did not agree with our lifestyle and then killed them.

God has once again called a living prophet, in our day, to help us get through these perilous times. I am grateful for this guidance and know that new revelation comes from God. Not only because I heard it from our current prophet, Gordon B. Hinckley, but because I received a confirmation by the Holy Ghost that he is a true prophet of God. This is the same way I knew that Joseph Smith also was a true prophet.

I felt that the true Church must have a living prophet and apostles, miracles, ministering of angels, priesthood authority from God and the restoration of all the power and spiritual gifts that were in operation during the time of ancient Judah and Jesus Christ. Now we have all of this. It is because of this confirmation that I knew that what I learned is true.

So here are powerful links to Judaism:

- The Book of Mormon together with the Bible fulfills the words of the ancient prophet Ezekiel to Israel.

- We now have a living prophet on the earth to guide and direct the Church just as the ancient Jews had prophets to guide and lead the Jewish Nation.

PATRIARCHAL BLESSING

All worthy members can also receive a patriarchal blessing. I received one, it was given to me by a special man, ordained by an Apostle of the Lord Jesus Christ, or one appointed by them, by laying his hands on my head and giving me the words of our Heavenly Father as a blessing which is recorded and written down. I was told many sacred things about my life on earth and my purpose here. I feel that this is the same blessing I received from my Heavenly Father before I left His presence in the premortal world. I will quote a few sentences from my blessing. "In the depths of your soul, you have often wondered who you were and desired to know the reality of your being. Now these things are being opened unto you, and this is pleasing to your spirit, which has sought light to fill the darkness of your understanding . . . The spirit within you is now peaceful, for you have found your God. The events of life and the promptings of the Lord have led you to your Savior Jesus Christ and his kingdom here on earth."

How perfectly these words described my life and experiences so far. These statements I knew were certainly true and were fulfilled at Rainbow Bridge, at my baptism, and later in the Lord's holy temple.

GOSPEL ALSO PREACHED
IN THE SPIRIT WORLD

One of the principles I was taught was that our Father in Heaven loves all of his children and provides an opportunity to every soul to hear and embrace His gospel. This includes even our grandfathers and grandmothers who have died before us without the gospel. They too may hear the gospel of Jesus Christ in the spirit world, and accept or reject it. Thus the gospel is preached in the spirit world after death by missionaries (see D&C 138:57) just as it is here on the earth. I know that in order to get into heaven, everyone must be baptized by authority. How can our dead kinsmen be baptized? As Paul said in 1 Corinthians 15:29 "Else what shall they do which are baptized for the dead if the dead rise not at all? Why are they then baptized for the dead?"

Our deceased ancestors cannot be baptized in the spirit world. Thus, our Father in Heaven, who loves all of His children, has provided a way for us to help our dead kinsmen gain entrance to His kingdom, if they agree. God instructed the Latter-day Saints to build temples where baptisms for the dead can be performed.

But there is more that is done in the temple. The ancient priesthood power to bind and seal on earth as well as in heaven has been restored from God to special priesthood holders in the Church. Because of this we can be vicariously married or "sealed," not only until death do us part, but for time and all eternity even after the resurrection. We are asked to find the names of our ancestors so they can be linked or bound to us in an eternal family. What a marvelous doctrine. It was sweet to my soul. I believe these doctrines were true for the living as well as the dead.

In the temple, we can remember and honor our ancestors. We can do these ordinances for and in behalf of them. That does *not* mean they are members of the Church, it means that if they decide to accept the gospel of Jesus Christ like I did, then they can do so and their temple ordinances become valid. *They still have free agency to accept or reject the gospel, even in the spirit world.*

The purpose of the temple also answered a profound question for me. The hearts of the children and the fathers can turn to one another (see Malachi 4:6). Why did so much of the Bible contain genealogies? Now I realized that it was important to God to maintain this information so that we could seal our families together back in time.

ENTERING THE TEMPLE

Before I was baptized, I received a brief explanation of the purpose of a modern temple. After I joined the Church, I learned much more about temples and their purpose. I was ready to ask for a special temple recommend from my bishop so that I could enter the house of the Lord to receive my endowment. "The Temple 'endowment'" gives me knowledge about my "eternal journey and limitless possibilities and progress which a just and loving Father [in Heaven]" can provide for His "children whom he made in his own image—for the whole human family" (*Teachings of Presidents of the Church*, David O McKay, pg 126).

On May 30, 1997, exactly one year after my baptism, I went to the temple to receive my endowment. I felt like an ancient Israelite walking into a true temple of God. A temple patterned after the one first built by Moses. For me, this was the fulfillment of all the ages of what my ancestors started so long ago. My mind felt at peace. I could feel the Spirit of the Lord surround and comfort me. I was now part of his great and eternal work and knew that His temple was sacred. I knew that this was truly the Lord's house on the earth, and I felt His Spirit dwelling there.

I walked into the Lord's house thinking about not only my salvation but that of all my ancestors that had died before me without the gospel. How many of them now yearned for the same opportunity that I had. How many of those precious souls had also received and understood the knowledge of Jesus Christ in the spirit world? How many had studied the same gospel that I had on the earth and accepted it? How could I help them now?

Why was this important to a Jewish girl and a Jewish people. Because the temple is the fulfillment of God's covenant with us, the power of Elijah to seal on earth and in the heaven was given to our living prophet who ordained special men in the Church with the authority to unite families forever in our temples. I understood that we could progress beyond this world into the celestial kingdom where our families would continue together for eternity. I loved this doctrine. It was more fully explained to me as follows: "As touching Abraham and his seed, out of the world they should continue; both in the world and out of the world should they continue as innumerable as the stars; or, if ye were to count the sand upon the seashore ye could not number them" (D&C 132:30).

Thus the same promise that God made to Abraham can now be given to us, Abraham's seed. The hearts of the children were turning to their fathers and the fathers to the children (Malachi 4:5–6). Our deceased ancestors' spirits still lived, and they reached out to us to be joined together as an eternal family. What greater joy could there be than to be sealed together as fathers, mothers, and children in all our generations?

As I walked the halls of the temple, I could feel not only the Spirit of the Lord, but I gained other spiritual knowledge as well. I could understand many plain and precious things that had been lost that now became clear to my mind. It is like taking a university course and gaining an advanced degree in spirituality. Each time I would go, I would gain more understanding. I felt a yearning for the welfare of my deceased ancestors and knew that I was responsible for finding their names so that we could be bound together as an eternal family by the authority of the holy priesthood and in the name of Jesus Christ.

I was given the privilege of working in the temple as a volunteer. I loved being there and never wanted to leave. When I was in the temple, the world outside was forgotten and God's peace filled my heart. I was in the house of the Lord, and I knew it.

Purpose of Bloody Sacrifices in the Old Testament

In the ancient temple, we had special ceremonies that only the Aaronic or Levitical Priesthood could officiate in. The congregation would bring offerings and participate in a holy feast afterward. The pattern of the tabernacle/temple service was revealed by God originally to Moses. We had bloody sacrifices and burnt offerings that included animals and farm products. I never understood why we did this. I have now learned that these ancient bloody sacrifices were in the *"similitude of the sacrifice of the Only Begotten of the Father"* (Moses 5:7, emphasis added). These ceremonies were intended to remind the people of the coming of the Messiah who would make the Atonement. Jesus Christ's blood did atone for our sins. He was the final and ultimate sacrifice. This purpose had been lost to us over the centuries. The knowledge of the sacrifice of the Messiah for the Jewish people and all the world was understood by the ancient prophets (see Isaiah 53:4–12), but now has largely been overlooked or forgotten.

The book of Moses shed an enormous light on this subject with this information:

> And he gave unto them commandments, that they [Adam and Eve] should worship the Lord their God, and should offer the firstlings of their flocks, for an offering unto the Lord. And Adam was obedient unto the commandments of the Lord.
>
> And after many days an angel of the Lord appeared unto Adam, saying: Why dost thou offer sacrifices unto the Lord? And Adam said unto him: I know not, save the Lord commanded me.
>
> And then the angel spake, saying: This thing is a similitude of the sacrifice of the Only Begotten of the Father, which is full of grace and truth.
>
> Wherefore, thou shalt do all that thou doest in the name of the Son, and thou shalt repent and call upon God in the name of the Son forevermore. [Moses 5:5–8]

So Adam and Eve were commanded to offer bloody sacrifices and they were told the purpose. These words were written in the book of Moses that had been one of the lost books omitted from Genesis.

This knowledge makes a great difference to me now. I realized that the words of our prophets from the beginning all pointed to the

Messiah, the Son of God, Jesus Christ.

I learned from the Book of Mormon that when our Messiah, Jesus Christ, would come, He would fulfill and complete the law of Moses with regard to bloody sacrifices.

The Book of Mormon provided me with answers.

> Therefore, it is expedient that there should be a great and last sacrifice, and then shall there be, or it is expedient there should be, a stop to the shedding of blood; then shall the law of Moses be fulfilled; yea, it shall be all fulfilled, every jot and tittle, and none shall have passed away.
>
> And behold, this is the whole meaning of the law, every whit pointing to that great and last sacrifice; and that great and last sacrifice will be the Son of God, yea, infinite and eternal. [Alma 34:13–14]

The people in the Book of Mormon followed the law of Moses until the time when Jesus Christ visited them after His death and Resurrection and told them this:

> Behold I am Jesus Christ the Son of God. I created the heavens and the earth, and all things that in them are. . . .
>
> I came unto my own, and my own received me not. And the scriptures concerning my coming are fulfilled.
>
> . . . for behold, by me redemption cometh, and in me is the law of Moses fulfilled.
>
> And ye shall offer up unto me no more the shedding of blood; yea, your sacrifices and your burnt offerings shall be done away, for I will accept none of your sacrifices and your burnt offerings.
>
> And ye shall offer for a sacrifice unto me a broken heart and a contrite spirit. And whoso cometh unto me with a broken heart and a contrite spirit, him will I baptize with fire and with the Holy Ghost. [3 Nephi 9:15–17, 19–20]

I now had the experience of being in a modern temple—a temple that should have been operating among the Jewish nations since the time of Moses, but our forefathers turned away from it. The temple is the house of the Lord. It points us to our immortality and eternal lives. It is operated under the direction of Jesus Christ, who gives instructions to our prophet and the holy Melchizedek Priesthood officers. This is the priesthood that was lost to us so long ago because of the wickedness of our forefathers in building the golden calf after being led out of bondage and even after witnessing so many miracles.

I can see now that many events in our Jewish history point to our Messiah: the blood that was smeared over the lintels so that the angel of death passsed over us in Egypt; the need for a sacrificial lamb; even the paschal lamb that we have on our dinner tables during Passover. All these are shadows of our Messiah to come.

I am grateful that the temple has been restored by God, in all its glory, in these latter days.

TIME TO REFLECT

It was time to reflect on all that I had just learned. I realized I was still Jewish. In fact, I felt more Jewish now after learning the fullness of the gospel. I understand now the future that God envisioned for Judah at Mt. Sinai. I understand why he was angry and the penalty we paid. We had to settle for less. We were given the lesser or Aaronic Priesthood with its carnal commandments instead of the higher or Melchizedek Priesthood with its ordinances of eternal lives and exaltation. We did not understand the need for our Messiah, Jesus Christ. We did not want to meet Him face-to-face and learn from Him. We were afraid. I picture in my mind, my ancestors at Mt. Sinai. The tablets of stone that Moses brought down, at first, containing the higher revelations, were destroyed because of the golden calf worship. I think our ancestors should have felt a great loss, not really understanding the significance of this event and its consequences. The law of Moses was then established which contained only the lesser or Aaronic Priesthood, but did point the people to the coming of Messiah.

God has promised to gather Israel and Judah again in the last days and restore to them the fullness of the gospel, the higher priesthood, and a restoration of the temple. I pray, like me, that they will rejoice in this glorious restoration which comes from God.

> And then shall they rejoice; for they shall know that it is a blessing unto them from the hand of God; and their scales of darkness shall begin to fall from their eyes; . . .
>
> And it shall come to pass that the Jews which are scattered also shall begin to believe in Christ; and they shall begin to gather in upon the face of the land . . . [2 Nephi 30:6–7]

I understand clearly my need for my Messiah, my Savior, Jesus Christ. I depend on Him to help me through this life and forgive my sins through my repentance and His Atonement. He is so courageous and loving. I owe Him my life.

I feel that everything in the scriptures points to helping us gain our immortality and eternal life with our Heavenly Father along with our families. Why else are we here? I learned that my journey on the earth was for this purpose. I now discover it is also God's purpose. I want to quote a statement by God to Moses to show what God's purpose is:

> For this is my work and my glory—to bring to pass the immortality and eternal life of man. [Moses 1:39]

Moses also knew our Lord, Jesus Christ. In the book of Moses, the full text of his meeting with God on Mt. Sinai is written:

> The words of God, which he spake unto Moses at a time when Moses was caught up in an exceedingly high mountain,
>
> And he saw God face to face and he talked with him, and the glory of God was upon Moses: therefore he could endure his presence.
>
> And God spake unto Moses, saying: Behold I am the Lord God Almighty, and Endless is my name; for I am without beginning of days or end of years; and is not this endless?
>
> And, behold, thou are my son; wherefore look, and I will show thee the workmanship of mine hands; but not all, for my works are

without end, and also my words, for they never cease.

And I have a work for thee, Moses, my son; and thou art in the similitude of mine Only Begotten; and mine Only Begotten is and shall be the Savior, for he is full of grace and truth; but there is no God beside me, and all things are present with me, for I know them all.

And he also gave me commandments when he called unto me out of the burning bush, saying: Call upon God in the name of mine Only Begotten and worship me. [Moses 1:1–4, 6, 17]

If the entire text of the book of Moses had been kept in the Old Testament, there would be no doubt that Jesus Christ was our Messiah, the Son of God. We would have known that this was part of our Jewish religion from the beginning. I wonder who removed these precious words from our sacred text?

So I look forward, not dwelling anymore on the past, for I understand the purpose of our ancient religion as it points us forward to our eternal lives together with our families in the celestial kingdom of God. What a glorious doctrine. What joy and happiness I now have as I understand what fulfillment and completion is now available for Judah and all the world.

CHAPTER 5

My First Mission, to the Family History Library in Salt Lake City, Utah
(1998–2001)

> *Again, the kingdom of heaven is like unto a merchant man, seeking goodly pearls: Who, when he had found one pearl of great price, went and sold all that he had, and bought it. [Matt. 13:45–46]*

BLESSINGS FOR MY BUSINESS

My life was so happy. I had been given so much by God. I had my own small business, a nice home, and wonderful friends. I asked one of the men of the priesthood of the Church to come to my office and dedicate my business to the Lord. Of course, I had to keep the commandments of God in my business affairs as well as my personal life. From the moment of this priesthood prayer of dedication, a spirit of peace and cooperation permeated my office and employees. We worked together better and our business increased. I had a new partner in my business and His name was my Heavenly Father. But I know that I had to do more than I was doing for the Lord.

I understood that God was active in my life not only on Sunday but all the time. He was interested in my company and every aspect of my life. As I asked Him for help I received it according to His will and in His way. I remember one time that I was having some problems with personalities with regard to a large real estate closing. Everyone was getting very upset. I tried everything that I could, but no one would listen. I closed my door and asked in prayer for Heavenly Father to help solve this problem and calm everyone down so we could work together toward a solution. To my joy, within thirty minutes everyone had calmed down and came to an agreement, and no one was upset anymore. I was very grateful as this incident involved my best clients.

One client, whom I worked with many years earlier, called me on the phone and said, "I was trying to decide who to give this business to and I kept hearing your name in my head so I want to send you this contract to work on for us."

Decision to Sell All and Move to Salt Lake City, Utah

The more I learned about the gospel and how God worked in my life, the more I wanted to help the Lord and His work. I had never been so happy in my life, and I knew it was because of the spiritual knowledge that I was receiving. So what should I do? I could continue to spread the gospel in Dallas, Texas or maybe go on a full-time mission.

So I decided to ask Heavenly Father what He wanted me to do. Late one evening, I got on my knees, and said, "Dear Father in Heaven, I wish to serve Thee for the rest of my life. You have given me the greatest gift I have ever had in my life, membership in Thy Church. You blessed me at Rainbow Bridge. I owe You everything. I am willing to sell my home, my business in Texas and do Thy work. What do You want me to do? Then I ended my prayer in the name of Jesus Christ, amen.

Within two weeks I met the person who eventually purchased my business. Someone knocked on the door of my house and asked if I would sell it. There was no for sale sign out front. It was a real estate agent representing someone who wanted to live next door to their friends who were my neighbors. My house was sold to these people. Soon I was free of these worldly entanglements.

I talked with my stake president and asked him if I should go on a full-time proselyting mission or do genealogy and temple work for my family. He told me that it was all one mission and suggested that I do genealogy.

So, in September of 1998, I moved to Salt Lake City, Utah.

Why genealogy? I wanted to learn how to find the names of my ancestors. I wanted an eternal family linked together, generation to generation. The only way I was able to find their names was doing research in the greatest genealogy library in the world located in Salt Lake City. So I flew to Salt Lake and rented an apartment. When I arrived, I was introduced to the mission president of the Family History Mission. I learned that I could be called as a missionary-volunteer for one year and work in the library full-time. I would receive thorough training on how to do this work and be able to find my ancestors and help others with their genealogy work as well. I prayed about this opportunity and decided that I should do it.

I completed the necessary paper work for a full-time mission for one year and received my mission call to the Family History Mission signed by our prophet, Gordon B. Hinckley. I knew that this was the right course for my life. I was part of a new and exciting adventure that was different from anything that I had experience so far.

It takes faith to make this type of change, especially when I was doing so well in Dallas. After all, I had spent over thirty years building my business, and now I sold it. I had the faith to ask God what I should do. Then events took place that led me to the decision to move to Salt Lake. I could not see ahead, but knew that it was time for this change in my life. I have never had any regrets that I made this choice.

Jewish Database and
Two and One-half Year Mission

The first day on my mission was exciting. I met three hundred other senior missionaries in the Family and Church History Mission who were all volunteers from across the world. Each of us was assigned to various departments in the mission according to our talents and the inspiration of the Lord to our Family History Mission president. These missionaries had left their homes to serve the Lord. All of us did this at our own expense, as all missionaries in our Church are volunteers and are not paid with money. There are other ways that God blesses us.

I was assigned to work in the US and Canada area of the Family History Library (FHL). We went through extensive training for the first month before we were allowed to help anyone at the library. We were continually updated and instructed on sources and methods.

I saw on the reference shelves, at the library, many books that had been compiled by the staff that helped with various aspects of genealogy. We had indexes for passenger records, research guides for every state, and various countries and other finding aids. I was discussing with one of the staff members the need for another reference guide book for Jewish research at the Family History Library.

Much to my amazement, the director of the library sent me a letter authorizing me to create a reference guide. So I set about compiling a database of all the specifically Jewish records held by the Family History Library. But how would I do this? What should it look like? My first idea was to create a very small booklet listing the Jewish records at the FHL. This reference book could be used by the missionaries, staff, and volunteers when patrons with Jewish ancestry came into the library. We had many Jewish people using our records.

I was given a small office cubicle, a computer that had access to the library catalog, and left to my own devices to do this work. Thankfully, my "office" was in the same room with the people in collection development. They provided needed information about the library catalog. I soon realized that this job was larger than I thought. We had a vast collection of Jewish records throughout the world in all locations and languages.

My year as a missionary was coming to an end, and I had not completed this work. So I asked to extend my missionary time for another year. I was granted permission and continued my work on the Jewish database.

Word got out to the Jewish community that I was working on this project. Gary, a prominent Jewish genealogist, came by my office one day and talked to me. He said, "Nancy, this database should be on the Internet so that all the Jewish people would have access to it." When he said these words, I realized that he was right. My vision of this project had been too small. It should not only be in the Family History Library in Salt Lake City, it should be on the Internet for the whole world.

So I discussed this idea with the director of the library. He, in turn, discussed it with his supervisors. The director contacted me, and a decision was made to donate the database to the International Association of Jewish Genealogical Societies (IAJGS) during their 20th International Jewish Genealogy Conference in July of 2000 scheduled in Salt Lake City, Utah. The IAJGS would be free to do what they wanted once they received the database. They could create a CD or put it on the Internet.

This international meeting was six months away, and I was still not finished with my research. Also, I was typing the information into a WordPerfect format, and this would not work if the information were to be put on the Internet. So what should I do? What type of software would be needed to search the database on a CD and the Internet? Would I have time to complete all the typing? It was now up to nine volumes in length containing the titles and brief information about thousands of specifically Jewish microfilmed records which could be researched by patrons searching for their ancestors' names.

I worked many long hours, and by this time had been a missionary at the FHL for over two years. The IAJGS did not know that we were going to present this gift to them at their conference.

Finally, the day arrived, July 9, 2000. The nine-volume set of books containing a list of over 4000 specifically Jewish records and the CD edition were ready for presentation.

Richard E. Turley, Jr., managing director of the Family and Church History Department in Salt Lake City, Utah was the keynote speaker at the opening ceremony of the International Jewish Genealogy Conference. He gave a magnificent one-hour talk. Then at the end of his talk, he showed a box containing my books and CD and announced the gift by the Utah Genealogical Society to the IAJGS of the entire database.

There were approximately 650 Jewish genealogists in attendance gathered from all over the earth. They all rose, clapped and shouted for joy. They were truly astonished at this gift. I was asked to come up to the podium and say a few words.

I remember looking at their faces. Many had tears in their eyes. I saw, not only the people that attended, but I could feel the presence of their deceased ancestors knowing that their names could more easily be found so they could be part of a family once again. I knew that this database would help many Jewish researchers for years to come. In my remarks, I thanked our Heavenly Father for all the help He gave in getting this work done.

But that was not the end of my involvement with this database. The IAJGS wanted to put the information on a CD that could be sold to the public. They also talked with "JewishGen" who had a web site and agreed to donate the information to them for their use. Finally, the CD was complete and sent out to the IAJGS to sell. JewishGen was also given the CD and did a brilliant job putting it on their website (www.jewishgen.org/databases/fhlc). What joy to see this information available to Jewish researchers worldwide.

As of August, 2005, over 100,000 people have used this on-line database on the JewishGen web site. IAJGS sold many of their CDs. My time and effort to create this database was given without compensation to me. It was done with love and in hopes that this information will assist Jewish genealogists find information on their ancestors.

I know that I did not do this work alone. There were many in the FHL that helped me, and I also had the blessings of the Lord. It was truly a joint effort.

I worked with many Jewish genealogists who came to the library. They felt the need to find the names of their families that perished in the Holocaust. I showed them databases that were dated prior to WWII so they could reconstruct the families whose memories should never be lost. I cannot think of any better way to honor those that died than to write down the names of their parents, grandparents, great grandparents, uncles, aunts, and cousins going as far back in time as possible. This was a labor of love.

But in doing this work with members or non-members, it was the same. Everyone was passionate about their work and anxious to find the names of those that died and came before them. Many felt a need to be linked with the past in a way that they could not explain.

Of course, I understand the meaning of this work, realizing the importance of linking families together forever.

The IAJGS Award 2001

Each year, the IAJGS presents achievement awards to recognize excellence. I was thrilled that at their 21st International Jewish Genealogy Conference in London, England on July 12, 2001, I was given an award for Outstanding Contribution via Electronic Media. I was sorry that I was not there to receive the award, and thank Howard Margol for accepting it for me.

An excerpt of the IAJGS web page where the CD is sold is described below: (http://www.iajgs.org)

Index of Jewish Records at the Family History Library

NOW AVAILABLE ON CD

An index of Jewish Records at the Family History Library with Folio Views ® search engine.

This CD includes the largest index of Jewish records—records on microfilm, on microfiche, and in print—ever compiled and produced on a CD.

The records referred to are located in the Family History Library in Salt Lake City, Utah. It took 18 months to compile, update, and finalize the InfoBase for the CD. This new InfoBase on CD will enable you to find the very best materials at the Family History Library for your specific research problem. After that, you can contact your local Family History Center to order in a copy of the microfilms, or microfiche.

The CD comprises an index of thousands of records of significant value to Jewish genealogical research, including hundreds of records not previously known or publicized, for example:

- A book containing an alphabetical list of persons sent to Siberian work camps from Lithuania, 1941–1952. It identifies the I.D. number, name, father's name, birth year, date sent, date released or died, and name of camp to which the person was sent

- Microfilm lists of
    - Emigrants NOT sailing on emigrant ships
    - A list of Jewish returnees
    - A list of those held back from emigration
    - A list of arriving emigrants (including a list of those sent by rail to Antwerp, Tetschen, Stralsund and Vandrup at the outbreak of WWI)
    - Emigrants from Kovno (Kaunas)
    - Jewish orphans from Russia
    - A locality index (alphabetical) to Lithuanian Jewish Vital Records as well as the film numbers for the actual records. Included are all microfilm numbers for Jewish records received from the Lithuanian Historical Archive as recently as January 2001 as well as links to keep up with additional records as they are acquired and appear in the Family History Library Catalog.

Outstanding Contribution via Electronic Media Award presented for the Index of Jewish Records in the FHL. The index created by Nancy provides a crucial key to unlocking the vast Jewish genealogical resources contained within the Family History Library. In addition to all of the generally-known records, Nancy located and made more accessible many Jewish records not previously known, including obscure records not otherwise easily found. The resultant index has been made available both through both CD/ROM and on the Internet.

CHAPTER 6

Marriage to Lynn M. Hilton
(2001)

Verily I say unto you, if a man marry a wife by my word, which is my law, and by the new and everlasting covenant, and it is sealed unto them by the Holy Spirit of promise . . . and it shall be said unto them—Ye shall come forth in the first resurrection; and if it be after the first resurrection, in the next resurrection; and shall inherit thrones, kingdoms, principalities, and powers, dominions, all heights and depths—then shall it be written in the Lamb's Book of Life . . . if ye abide in my covenant . . . it shall be done unto them in all things whatsoever my servant hath put upon them, in time, and through all eternity; and shall be of full force when they are out of the world; and they shall pass by the angels, and the gods, which are set there, to their exaltation and glory in all things. [D&C 132:19]

SEARCHING FOR MY HUSBAND

I said earlier that sometimes we do good things in life without knowing what blessings we will receive from our Father in Heaven. I wanted to serve Him and volunteered for two and one-half years as a missionary working in the Family History Library. The result of that job was astonishing to me. The creation of the Jewish database was a great achievement, because I knew that it would help so many others. I could not see ahead, but God could.

Many of us think that blessings from God are for security, comfort, financial, and health. But I know that there are many more ways that our Father in Heaven can bless us if we are faithful.

I had been single for almost ten years and finally decided that it was time for me to find a husband and be sealed (married) in the temple for time and all eternity. But I wanted to find the man that was described in my patriarchal blessing, a high priest, truly a faithful son of God. So I prayed to Heavenly Father about this for a year. I know I was in no position to do anything about a husband as I was a missionary serving in the FHL but I would soon be finished and maybe some future plans could be made by my Father in Heaven to answer my prayers.

I had learned enough about the gospel and the power of prayer to understand that I had to ask. I knew that God knew what I wanted, but I had to ask! And I had to be specific in what I asked for. Then I left it up to my Heavenly Father.

My patriarchal blessing had given me this promise, "I bless you to go there [the temple] one day and be married for time and eternity to one of the Lord's choice sons. I bless you that this will be the fulfillment of the happiness, joy and peace of soul you have desired. I bless you with eternal companionship and eternal friendship with one holding the sacred powers of the holy Priesthood; truly, a faithful son of God. You shall come to understand the celestial nature of the eternal sealings and bindings to companion, to family and to your God. I bless you that joy, peace and comfort will abound in your home and family, and that your whole being will be lifted to great heights."

Introduced by Jess and Patti Shumway

Toward the end of my mission, I met Patti and Jess Shumway who were also working as missionaries in the Family History Library where I was. Patti and I became good friends. We loved to go on walks together, in City Park, to get exercise. In September 2000, during one of our walks, Patti told me about her brother Lynn and what an exceptional man he was. She invited me to a family home evening in her home in Provo, Utah to hear her brother give a talk. I remember the first time I met him. (See his picture on page 112.) He was tall and very handsome with a touch of white hair at his temples, a beautiful smile and kind eyes. He gave a talk on evidence found at the likely crossing site where Moses opened the Red Sea. He showed pictures of chariot wheels that were found under the Red Sea by Ron Wyatt. He also talked about his trip to Jerusalem. I was so astonished at his knowledge. I thought to myself, *If only he were younger.* Lynn told me later, that he thought, *If only she were older.* There is an age difference, but we laugh about it now. For in the eternities, age will not matter.

I learned that Lynn has a PhD degree from the University of Chicago in Educational Administration. He was Associate Dean of Adult Education at Brigham Young University for twelve years. He was a pioneer and started many programs that are operating today such as the off-campus adult education centers, Travel Study Department, Know Your Religion lectures, the evening schools and assisted in the formation of the BYU center in Jerusalem. Later he was also a legislator as well as a successful business man.

Lynn was truly a pioneer and was called on a mission in 1975 to find the original Lehi trail which was written up in the *Ensign* magazine in the September and October 1976 editions. I read his latest book, published in 1996 entitled *Discovering Lehi*. It is a marvelous book and is currently in Latter-day Saint bookstores.

Patti and Jess also arranged for us to meet again at various other firesides and missionary events. I enjoyed talking to Lynn, but we had only brief conversations. In December 2000, I was sitting at home reading the scriptures when I heard the name Lynn Hilton repeated inside of my mind several times. This occurred quite often over the next few weeks. Finally, I went to the temple and asked my Heavenly Father, in prayer, why I was hearing the name of Lynn Hilton. I received a confirmation from the Lord that I was going to marry Lynn M. Hilton. I was so astonished. I asked God to allow me to feel as he did about Lynn. I immediately felt a huge amount of love. Because of this feeling I felt the same love for Lynn. I had barely known him but already knew that I loved him.

I remember that at one of the firesides that Patti had invited us both to attend, Lynn told me that he had a dream about me. Lynn also told me that his first wife Hope had died a year and one-half earlier. She had been sick and had a slow death over a period of five years. He said that this event had taken a toll on his own health.

Lynn later told me that a year before Hope died he met a good friend in the temple who told him that after Lynn's wife died, "You will have a new life, a new wife, and a new mission!" Later, after her passing, he remembered these words and thought to himself, *Well, I'd better do something about this and start looking for a new wife.*

He made a list of eighteen names of faithful women he knew and started calling each one to take them to dinner or the opera. Patti asked him to put my name on the list. He was reluctant to do this as he thought that I was too new in the Church and he was not sure of the depth of my faith. He really wanted a wife that had been born in the Church. In order to please his sister, he did as she requested.

It was then that Patti decided that it was time to act. She called her brother and said to him, "Lynn, I think you should marry Nancy." He said, "Oh, why is that?" Patti said, "Because the Spirit of the Lord told me you should." Lynn told me later, that when she said those words, it was like hearing a thunder bolt. At the same instant he also received a confirmation from the Lord that we should marry. He said that a great burden instantly lifted off his shoulders and he knew his search was finished and we would be married and sealed in the temple if I would agree. He said he saw a long, straight road ahead and at the end of the road was a bright light. He knew his quest to find a wife was over.

But Patti, said, "Lynn, you have to court her and win her love." He said to her, "How do I do that?" The next day was Valentine's Day, and Lynn had plans to visit Patti in the Family History Library. Patti told me that he was coming and that I should expect something wonderful. Lynn showed up with a box of chocolates and also gave me a silver honey bee. The bee, he explained, was the symbol of Zion, the city of our God. I was so touched. We knew that this was the first step in learning about each other. I remember looking into his beautiful eyes and feeling such love that it filled my entire heart. I was never so happy in my life. When I came home to my apartment that night I found a bouquet of a dozen red carnations outside of my door. I was touched by his thoughtfulness.

That night and every night thereafter we talked for hours on the phone. He came, often to visit me in the Family History Library as I was still on a mission. We also went to the temple at the same time, and that time together was special.

Marriage Proposal

On the day I was released from my mission, Lynn was waiting outside of my mission president's door. Patti was there also with a camera. When I emerged with my honorable release, she took our picture along with the mission president and his wife.

After that, Lynn and I walked to my apartment. Lynn read me Doctrine and Covenants 132:19 about eternal marriage. He told me that was the kind of marriage he wanted for us. Then he got on his knees and asked me to marry him. I said, "Yes." This engagement was done within an hour of my release as a missionary. I was so thrilled. I was never so happy in my life.

Telling My Parents

But how would I tell my family? They did not know about Lynn. I had never even indicated that I was interested in anyone. Lynn and I decided that we were going to be married in two months time, and then we planned to put in our papers and go on a Latter-day Saint senior mission together. He had promised me that we would go on not less than five missions together.

I called my home, and my mother answered the phone. I told her that I had great news; I was getting married. Her reaction was to be expected. She said, "What!!! Who is this person?"

So I handed the phone to Lynn and said to him, talk to my mother. He gave me a big smile and introduced himself to my parents for the first time. He then sent them a huge bouquet of flowers. My parents' hearts softened as they got to know Lynn and were happy for me.

Meeting Lynn's Children and Grandchildren

Lynn is a very special man. He is so loving, kind, brilliant, adventurous, and faithful to the Church and the Lord. He is the greatest man I have ever met. My love grows everyday that I am with him. I am so thankful that I will be married to him for time and all eternity; not until death but forever.

Lynn has four married children and fourteen grandchildren. I was concerned about their acceptance of me. I must say that I have never felt so much love from a family in my life. His daughter, Sheree, was the first one I met. She came to the Family History Library and we talked. She is so beautiful, and I felt an instant love for her. I felt this way about each of his children. They are marvelous, bright, kind, and loving. The next person I met was Barbara, the wife of his son Ralph. She was working as a nurse. She told me that Lynn was a very special man and that he was a lot of fun to be with. Barbara was so kind to me. I knew that I would love being part of Lynn's family.

All of Lynn's grandchildren are wonderful. How blessed I was to be accepted. This was a fulfillment of the words in my patriarchal blessing that I would be married in the temple to a faithful son of God. And my home would be full of joy and peace. I could not thank my Heavenly Father enough for this great gift—this marvelous blessing.

Temple Marriage and Sealing in the Salt Lake Temple

We wrote out the names of family and friends to be invited to our wedding planned for the temple in Salt Lake City. There were so many people we wanted to invite that the list grew and grew. We decided to have a big wedding and invite everyone.

The day of our wedding approached. All the arrangements had been made. My parents arrived a day early, and Lynn and I went to pick them up at the airport. My dad had not been well. I was so happy to see them. They met Lynn for the first time. Both of them loved him. Lynn said he was old-fashioned and asked my father for his permission to marry me. I thought that was very special. My father, in a formal, dignified way, said that he gave his permission.

I had a brief opportunity to talk to my father before our wedding. I thanked him for coming as I knew that it was difficult for him to walk, and he was not feeling very well. He said, "I would not have missed your wedding even if I had to crawl to come." His love and his words touched my heart in a way that I can only describe with tears, even today. Mother also loved Lynn and poured out her love to us. I was so grateful to them. Lynn loved them also. My brother and his wife came to our wedding. It was wonderful that they were all there.

I remember at the dinner Lynn gave at the Lion House the night before our wedding, I looked at everyone that was there. We had my precious Jewish family, my mother, dad, brother, and his wife. We had Lynn's family, his children, and grandchildren. All my missionary friends from the library were also there that I had grown so close to. Lynn's sister Patti and her husband Jess were there. I thought, this is the way it should be. I could feel the love that permeated every heart no matter our backgrounds. This is the true gospel of Jesus Christ— to love one another. I also looked at my future husband with such profound gratitude to my Heavenly Father for his help in bringing this to pass. I know that I could not have found Lynn by myself.

Our wedding day finally arrived, May 26, 2001. We had to be in the temple by 6:30 a.m. for our wedding at 8:00 a.m. Patti and Lynn's son Ralph went with us to the temple to help us get ready. Lynn and I were dressed in white. I wore a beautiful temple dress that I purchased for the occasion. We met at the sealers' office and signed the necessary papers. We had already obtained a marriage license from the State of Utah, County of Salt Lake, but now we would receive a marriage document confirming our eternal marriage in the temple.

When we walked into the sealing room, it was filled with about ninety of our family and friends. It was truly packed. We also felt the presence of many spirits from the other side in attendance. If we had eyes to see, we think that we could have seen our deceased ancestors who were there as well as many angels.

During the sealing ceremony, I could feel the depth of our love as we looked into each other's eyes. I felt the love of our Heavenly Father pour into our hearts, and we breathed a sigh that cannot be described in words. I understood that I was eternally bound to my husband, our families, and my God.

I know that some day, as we sit side by side, thousands of years from now, we will remember this day with gratitude and love that we lived in a time when we could partake of this great blessing.

After the ceremony, I put on a beautiful wedding dress, and Lynn wore a tuxedo with a white jacket. He was so handsome. Outside the temple we took wedding pictures. One of Lynn's friends had a video camera and was filming us. We had hired a photographer. I was never so happy in my life.

My mother had arranged to give a brunch for the family. So after we finished taking the pictures, we gathered together to have some food. That was so nice of my parents to do this for us. Then Lynn and I went to prepare for the reception that took place a few hours later in the Joseph Smith Memorial Building. Everything was perfect that day. The reception was attended by hundreds of our friends and family. Lynn and I stood in line greeting our guests for hours. Finally all the festivities were finished, and we all went home. I was now Mrs. Lynn M. Hilton. What joy!

Since that day I have reflected on this event and rejoice in the love that we have for each other. I have eternal companionship and eternal friendship with one holding the sacred powers of the holy priesthood, truly, a faithful son of God. I have great joy, peace, and comfort in my home with a family that is now mine. I will be with Lynn forever. What greater blessing from God can there be than this?

FOREIGN TRAVEL

Lynn is so adventurous. He has traveled throughout the world. I had hardly ever traveled, so we decided to go on some trips. The first place we visited was Lithuania. We were invited by Howard Margol, the president of the IAJGS, to join his Jewish genealogical tour of Lithuania. In addition to visiting the archives for research, we also went to the sites of the Jewish massacres and ghettos in Vilnius and other areas of Lithuania. Many thousands of Jews from Lithuania perished during WWII. There are huge burial pits all over the countryside that contain the bodies of these precious Jewish people. One pit near Vilnius contained over 60,000 Jewish bodies. When Lynn and I went to these places, we could feel the despair and darkness of spirit that permeated the area. My precious husband said a prayer of faith for them, and I felt comforted.

Lynn and I will never forget this trip. Our emotions overflowed as we considered what had happened to Judah here. Our hearts were drawn out in much faith, dedication, and blessings on their behalf. We felt the love of the Lord and that he accepted our prayers. We will never forget this trip for it touched our hearts in a profound way.

A few months later we went on a BYU tour of Central America to see the ruins likely connected to the Book of Mormon. We visited Guatemala, Honduras, Belize and the Yucatan. This was a great trip. We gave away 46 copies of the Book of Mormon in Spanish in two weeks time. The people in these countries are so receptive to the message of the Book of Mormon because it is a record of their own history.

The Hilton Family Reunion

The Hilton family had planned a reunion in Woodruff, Arizona where Lynn's mother was raised. Lynn had six brothers and one sister. His brothers George, Ted, Phil, and his sister Patti, and their families were in attendance. I was thrilled to meet the members of this great family. All of the other brothers had passed away, but their families were there also.

My heart was filled with joy as I now knew that I was part of a large family—one that not only was present at this family reunion but stretched back into time beyond the veil of death and into the eternities. Our families, both Jewish and Mormon, were united and joined together in a way that I could not have understood just a few years earlier. Through the Atonement and Resurrection of Jesus Christ and the Restoration of His Church all of this was possible.

When we returned home, we decided it was time to get serious about our missions that we wanted to do for the Church, so we put in our papers for an eighteen month mission and agreed that we would go wherever the Lord sent us.

CHAPTER 7

Mission with Elder Lynn M. Hilton to Sydney, Australia
(2002–2003)

> *That ye may be prepared in all things when I [the Lord] shall send you again to magnify the calling whereunto I have called you, and the mission with which I have commissioned you. Behold, I sent you out to testify and warn the people, and it becometh every man who hath been warned to warn his neighbor. [D&C 88:80–81]*

THE LETTER FROM OUR PROPHET INCLUDED OUR MISSION CALL

The day arrived when we received an envelope with our mission call. Lynn and I sat down at our dining room table and opened the envelope together. We had been asked to serve in Sydney, Australia as regional employment specialists for eighteen months. We were to start our mission on March 4, 2002, about three months from the date we received this letter.

MY FATHER'S DEATH

My father had been ill, and we made it a priority to spend time with him and my mother before we left on our mission. We went on a special Caribbean cruise, as a family, in December with my parents, my brother, and his wife. It was a special time being together as a family. My dad was still able to get around, but very slowly. He was very thin and weak, but his mind was alert even though his body was deteriorating.

After the cruise, we had to get ready to go on our mission and had much to do before we left. In the middle of February, both of us felt strongly that we needed to return to Florida to see my parents one more time. We got on a plane and flew down there. When we arrived, it did not appear that Dad was doing worse, but within one day of our arrival things started happening very quickly, and he could no longer stand up on his own. So Lynn and I moved into my parents' small apartment and tried to help Dad. Lynn served as his nurse. Within another day we had hospice there evaluating him. They said they would supply nurses that would be there twenty-four hours a day. I know that these women who work for hospice are the best, kindest, unselfish, and most loving people I have ever met. Dad got worse everyday, and we had to get a hospital bed, wheelchair, and other items to assist him. The hospice nurses said that he was deteriorating quickly.

Lynn had to go home and finalize our packing and other items that we needed to do before we left for Australia. I stayed another week with Mom and Dad and the nurses. I did not get much sleep. Dad slept a lot. I learned about the different stages of dying from a small booklet I was given by hospice. My Father was going through all of them. He would say to me, "I am dying. I am dying."

One night as I was sitting beside my father's bed, he woke up and said, "I want to die. I want to die." I asked him why he was saying that. He told me, "I have been in another place. A place that was beautiful, peaceful, and without pain; but, when I awoke I was back here."

The time I spent with my father and mother during those days and nights can only be described as precious. I drew closer to my parents than I had ever before. I said many prayers and felt the comfort of the Spirit. I remember standing in the doorway watching my father when I felt a great love for him. I was not afraid for him as I felt a spiritual presence, possibly his ancestors, who had come to escort him into the spirit world at his death. He had a close call that evening but was given oxygen to help him breathe, so he lingered on.

After my return home, Dad was moved to a nursing care facility across the street from where Mom lived. Mom said he was doing a little better but still refused to eat. Then I got word right before we were to go into the Missionary Training Center that he had passed away. My sadness was tempered with the thought that his body might be dead but not his spirit. That he lived on as my Dad, in the spirit world where he would hear the gospel from missionaries there and hopefully embrace its truths as I had. My precious brother was also with Dad before he died and with Mom afterward. My parents had been married sixty-six years at the time of my father's death.

Arrival in Sydney Australia

Lynn and I arrived in Sydney, Australia on March 15, 2002. Our mission was for eighteen months. We felt inadequate for the task and did not know how to do our job. Our area of work was New South Wales. Our job was to provide employment assistance for 30,000 Latter-day Saints in ten stakes and 76 wards. We had wards that were Samoan, Tongan, Chinese, and Spanish as well as Australian. Many of the meetings in these wards were in their native tongue.

Our apartment or flat, located on the third floor of an apartment building, was very small but adequate. We lived in one of twenty units in two apartment buildings owned by the Church. All the occupants were senior missionaries except for the manager who also worked at the area office.

The next day our supervisor, the area welfare agent, drove us, on the left side of the road, to our employment office that had been established in a brand new stake building located a forty-five minute drive from our apartment. *How will we ever find this place again,* ran through my mind? So I marked in the map book our route and wrote some notes so we could find our office again.

Creating an Employment Program

So what should we do on our mission? How could we help our members? We were left to our own devices. We sat in our employment office for a few days without anyone coming and decided that would not work. We knew that employment was a challenge especially to our foreign members who did not speak or read English.

Here is how it worked. We did our homework and read everything we could find on employment. We talked with the stake employment specialists so we could understand the needs of our members. Then we would pray and receive inspiration with a concept or idea. Once we understood the concept, then we, mostly Lynn, would create a written document that matched the idea. I was great on the computer. Then we would tweak (change) the document many times before we felt it was acceptable. As these documents and ideas were given to us, we could feel the presence of the Spirit increasing our knowledge and giving us new ideas. It was truly a wonderful partnership with the two of us and the Lord. The Lord does not do our work for us. We have to do our part and *ask* Him for specific help.

Speaking in Sacrament, Relief Society, and Priesthood Meetings about Employment

Over the next six months we created an adult career handout as well as the youth program. We planned a presentation for each of the seventy-six wards. The ward employment presentation included our speaking in sacrament meeting, priesthood and Relief Society about employment. We realized that talking about employment during church meetings is not a sin. It is an important part of the gospel. If we help each other, we can grow economically and also receive spiritual blessings. This builds faith.

We talked to the members about job coaching, networking with each other, filling out job opening sheets, and letting each other know about jobs being available. We taught them about interviewing, describing themselves in thirty seconds, telephoning, and many other employment skills. We learned about the school system, free English classes, and scholarships. We prepared a web site list for the Australian job market, schools, and employment opportunities and included that in our handouts. We could see that if the members of the Church helped each other, we could all prosper.

One story that Lynn told very often during our time in Sydney has to do with learning by "study and faith" (D&C 109:7). This story illustrates how our Father in Heaven helps us with new inventions and knowledge. How many times have we tried to figure out a problem and then suddenly a solution or new idea "pops" into our mind. This inspiration is from God. I had never realized how much God helps us in this life with new ideas, inventions, and knowledge.

Lynn related this story about his brother, "George Hilton was an eye surgeon. His specialty was doing surgery to reattach detached retinas. But the procedure was difficult for the patient and took a long time to recover. He had to cut the eye open, find the retina and sew it back into place. He had studied all there was on this subject and had all the latest techniques and knowledge. He prayed to God to help him find a better way. At this time he was a bishop in his ward. He related to Lynn that one day he was in his back yard doing carpentry work on his fence. He was holding up a spirit level to see if the board was level when he heard the promptings of the Spirit. He focused on the bubble in the level and the Holy Spirit said, in his mind, would it be possible to inject a bubble of gas into the eye? Then you could turn the patient around in such a way to get the bubble under the retina, and it would push it back into place. You can then use a laser to weld the retina into place. George realized that this was the inspiration he needed. He went to work perfecting this technique. This technique is now used throughout the world. George had to do the work, learn all that he could, and then ask the Lord for what he still lacked. This inspiration has helped many people." This is what is meant by "get learning by study and by faith" (D&C 88:118).

Youth Career Workshop

One young Latter-day Saint man who had quit school in the tenth grade, then completed a mission, came to us after he heard us speak in the youth career class. He wondered what we thought he should do for a living. We both told him instantly he should be a lawyer. He said he went home and prayed about it and felt the same way. So this young man along with two of his friends started planning their lives to become lawyers. We recently heard from him. He is currently at the university taking courses so he can achieve his goal. He is also teaching the youth career workshop in his stake.

Better Employment in Building Up the Kingdom of God

Lynn and I learned what it is to be a senior couple working for the Lord. We received blessings not only individually but as a couple or team working together for the good of our Father's children. The program that we were inspired to start was not planned or provided for in Salt Lake but grew little by little, line upon line, as we worked together to meet the local needs in Australia. Lynn and I grew close together and learned unity and what it is to be one with each other and the Lord.

We also learned the importance of employment in building up the Lord's kingdom. We heard many stories from the members when we talked in Relief Society and priesthood. One story, I will always remember. I asked the Relief Society sisters if they would share a story about how Heavenly Father helped them in their employment.

One sister told us that she was a nurse. She decided that she should study to become a midwife. After she started the course, she realized that it was too hard for her to learn, and she would have to quit. She decided to pray about it before quitting because she had felt inspired to become a midwife. After her prayer, she heard these words, "I need you to become a midwife as your talents will be needed in the latter days." She told us that she was astonished to hear these words as she did not realize until that moment that her employment had a higher purpose. She told us that she talked to our Father in Heaven and asked Him to help her remember and understand how to do the work of a midwife and help her with her school work. She told us that she received this help, from the Spirit. What a great testimony of the importance of employment. I know that Heavenly Father is interested in our employment and that He will help us if we are faithful. I knew this was true from my own experiences.

Thus, I came to understand that every aspect of my life was of interest to my Father in Heaven. He knew of me even before I was able to converse with Him. His words thundered into my mind at Rainbow Bridge, but now His quiet inspiration, through prayer, and His impressions on my mind, became a vital and living part of my everyday life. I strive to keep the commandments so that I can continue, through the Holy Ghost, to feel His presence in my life.

Through the many faithful testimonies we heard from our members regarding their school work, employment, and family life, we realized the huge extent that our Father in Heaven is active in their lives.

We met people from all walks of life, different socio-economic conditions, and different cultures; but everyone in the Church learns the same gospel. I heard the gospel in Dallas. They heard it in Samoa, Tonga, Australia, Sri Lanka, New Zealand and Papua New Guinea. What a testimony that God lives and is the same God for everyone.

Working in the Sydney Temple

We were also blessed to have a temple in Sydney, Australia. We were asked to be temple ordinance workers on Thursday nights. Working in the temple with my husband and other temple ordinance workers was a joy. It is truly like living in the celestial kingdom.

It is different going to the temple as a patron and going as an ordinance worker. The spiritually that I felt was strengthened, and I drew closer to my Father in Heaven. The temple is a place where heaven and earth meet together; where work is done by the living for the dead in the most loving way. Miracles happen often and joy abounds.

Family History Work in Sydney

Doing family history work is always important, and we promoted this on our mission as well. We worked with a sister missionary from Papua New Guinea. She could barely read or write, as she grew up in a village in the forest. Her parents died very young, and she was raised by her sister who was also a member of the Church. The day after she dictated the names of her deceased ancestors from memory on to a pedigree chart, she told us she had a dream where hundreds of her deceased family came to her sister's home in Papua New Guinea and ate all the food that she had cooked. She understood that the dream was about her deceased ancestors who were learning the gospel (eating her food) and wanting to get their temple work done. She told us that when she did the work for her parents in the temple, that they were there, in the spirit, with her. She was so thrilled.

The End of Our Australian Mission

We were sad to leave Australia and our mission field. We had learned so much and had grown in ways that we could not have done if we had stayed in Salt Lake City. We forgot ourselves, and allowed the Lord to lead and guide our mission. We saw His hand in this work and we grew closer together. I know that there is no other way that we could have learned these lessons as a couple. I understand why it is so important to go on a senior mission if it is possible. It is truly a training ground for the celestial kingdom.

We also had a lot of fun and met the best people who are our eternal friends. Our mission was wonderful. My understanding of the living gospel of Jesus Christ grew in ways that are difficult to detail. I realized that through the spiritual events that took place on this mission that I had changed again and again. My faith in the Lord grew as I could see Him helping His children in ways that I previously never considered possible. We heard testimonies from our fellow Latter-day Saint members about the promptings of the Spirit in their lives, their jobs, and their schoolwork.

I understood the gospel in a new way that it could help us toward practical and financial success in our mortal lives. We are taught that faith leads to action. I know that is true. If we think of the Lord as our friend and partner, then our life on the earth becomes enriched with miracles and spiritual guidance. This is a way for the Lord to prosper us as He has promised. But we must ask for His help in a specific way and do our part.

CHAPTER 8

Second Mission with Elder Hilton, Employment Section of the Church Welfare Department

(2003-2004)

> *And now I would that ye should be diligent in keeping the commandments of God at all times; asking for whatsoever things ye stand in need, both spiritual and temporal [including employment and schooling] always returning thanks unto God for whatsoever things ye do receive. [Alma 7:23]*

WORKING TOGETHER WITH THE EMPLOYMENT TEAM

Upon our return to Salt Lake, we were asked to give a report of our work in Sydney, Australia to the Employment Department at Church headquarters. Because of our innovative work, we were asked to create and make recommendations for an employment program for the wards and stakes for the entire Church. This was a Church service mission.

The headquarters and staff for the program is located in the employment section of the Church's Welfare Department located on the seventh floor of the Church Office Building, Salt Lake City, Utah, USA. We became well acquainted with each one of these marvelous, bright, and dedicated people. Our program had to include a variety of qualifications that we had not previously considered. The most important of which is that this new program had to work throughout the entire Church, in all countries and cultures. We were provided direction and met regularly with our supervisor and the director of the Employment Department. We met and talked with many of the employment directors of the various centers throughout the world and received feedback on our proposed program.

Wrote the Suggested LDS Employment Program for Wards and Stakes

We worked on this project for ten months. Based on our work in Sydney, we suggested that the employment program should be taken to each member in the ward. We outlined various steps that could be implemented Church-wide to help our members gain better employment and education. The key to better employment was helping each other by utilizing the talents of our members in networking and job coaching.

I learned three major things during our employment missions:

- I know the importance of school and employment in building up God's kingdom on the earth and how our Father in Heaven helps us. For "Whatever principle of intelligence we attain unto in this life, it will rise with us in the resurrection" (D&C 130:18).

- We cannot do this work alone. It requires the talents of all the members and the dedicated staff that work in Church headquarters. As we grow in understanding of the true and full gospel of Jesus Christ we can learn together, work together, and help each other gain our exaltation in the celestial kingdom of God. It takes effort and faith.

- Heavenly Father inspires men and women across this vast earth with knowledge to invent new products that can help humanity. It might not be recognized as coming from Him but it is true none the less. I realized that many times I was trying to find an answer or solution to a problem that I had studied and suddenly the answer came like a light bulb turning on. This inspiration is from God and helps us find solutions when the earthly knowledge we need is too limited or does not yet exist. I wonder how many times I said, "Ah ha! That is the answer!" as if I had something to do with the solution. I want to thank our Heavenly Father for this help in our lives. Spiritual knowledge and temporal knowledge are both important. They are interconnected. They both come from God.

Lynn and I finished this mission the day before we left for our third mission.

CHAPTER 9

Third Mission with Elder Hilton, Greece Athens Mission, Part One, Irbid Jordan
(2004–2005)

And if it so be that you should labor all your days in crying repentance unto this people, and bring, save it be one soul unto me, how great shall be your joy with him in the kingdom of my Father!

And now, if your joy will be great with one soul that you have brought unto me into the kingdom of my Father, . . . how great will be your joy if you should bring many souls unto me! [D&C 18:15–16]

MISSION CALL TO GREECE ATHENS MISSION IN IRBID, JORDAN

In November of 2003 we put in our mission papers again for another full-time, eighteen-month mission. We received our calling in December to work in the Greece Athens Mission under the direction of our mission president. I remember when we put in our papers indicating that we would work wherever the Lord assigned us, I thought to myself, *I do not want to go to the Middle East*. Well, when we received this calling, we looked up the boundaries of this mission. They included the countries of Jordan, Syria, Lebanon, Egypt, Greece, and Cyprus. We heard from our mission president that he wanted us to go to Jordan. I was a little afraid as I was Jewish. So Lynn and I decided that we would never say a word about my background to anyone, even the other senior missionaries. We would put our trust in the Lord and serve in a Muslim nation exactly as we had been called to do.

Elder Lynn M. Hilton and Sister Nancy Hilton, 2005
Picture taken by Vasilis Haralampopoelos, Athens, Greece

OVERCOMING PERSONAL FEELINGS OF FEAR

We left Salt Lake on April 15, 2004 and flew into Athens, Greece. We spent the night at the mission home and then flew into Amman, Jordan the next day. If I was to tell you that I felt at ease I would be lying. This was a world that was so foreign to me. My husband had lived in Egypt and Saudi Arabia for many years and could speak some Arabic. He knew the culture and how to talk to the people. The signs were all in Arabic, the people looked very different to me, and I was scared. I clung to Lynn for a lifeline.

We were met by the senior couples who lived in Amman and Al Husn, or north Jordan. They piled our luggage into their cars and off we went to the Amman Center. We then went on to north Jordan to start our work there. My first impression of Jordan was beautiful scenery. There is something so unique and wonderful about Jordan. It is hard to define, but it is a place of great beauty. It is a land where the Savior was baptized and walked its dusty roads.

So here I am, in a predominately Muslim nation of five million people, of which five percent are Christian. The first night I was there I was awakened by the call to prayer at 4:30 a.m. I sat up in bed listening to the sound and said to myself, "What am I doing here?"

Usually one mosque would start the prayer, and then others would follow like an echo over the nation.

After a few weeks, my mind tuned out the sound, and it became part of the rhythm of life as we went about our work.

Our apartment was very large. My first challenge was water. We could not drink the water, and it was also in short supply. In fact we ran out of water twice the first few months we were there. There was a problem filling our water tank on the roof from the city water that came in only once a week. This was finally solved, but we never used it for drinking. It was all right for bathing. We had to bring in bottled water to drink and cook with. All the food had to be sterilized using Clorox water. I am so grateful for Clorox. The grocery store had a variety of food that I did not recognize nor understand how to use because I could not read the directions. But this soon became routine, and we did not have any physical problems or illness while we lived in Jordan. I will say that we always said a blessing before we ate and asked Heavenly Father to bless the food and make sure that it would not harm us.

Lynn and I kept a journal of our thoughts and experiences in this land. Journals of each of our missions are large and detailed. We have them in our Salt Lake City apartment, but intend to donate them to Special Collections, Marriott Library, University of Utah, Salt Lake City, USA in the Lynn M. Hilton file.

We met many Arab Christian people. They were warm and friendly. They invited us into their homes and hearts. I fell in love with them even though I could not speak their language. The Spirit was so powerful and taught them when I could not. Our eyes would communicate and spirit would speak to spirit. I felt an immediate bond with a few of the women I met, both Christian and Muslim. There was a recognition that could come only from our friendship in the premortal existence. When this occurred, I felt a strong connection to our Father in Heaven whose love reaches into each heart and transcends the boundaries of speech and culture.

This was the same love that I felt from God at Rainbow Bridge, again when I married Lynn, and now when I looked into the eyes of Heavenly Father's children in Jordan.

The Christian women did not wear head scarves. Most of them did wear a cross, and that was quite a religious statement to make in a Muslim country. To them the cross was not just jewelry; it was a declaration of their belief in Jesus Christ. Al Husn, at one time, was all Christian. Now it was about fifty percent.

My husband Lynn was so kind and helpful. He understood my fears and helped me learn the language and reach out to the people. He was not afraid but would go forth and talk with the street vendors, store owners, and anyone else with a friendly Marhaba (hello) and a big smile. I soon relaxed and joined in.

Living in Al Husn was always full of surprises. We would walk out our door and see a shepherd with his sheep and goats wandering down the street. This became a common occurrence and one that I loved to see. We would see men riding heavily laden donkeys next to cars and taxis zooming by. Most people had no cars, so transportation was limited to walking, the bus, and taxis. Jordan is a mixture of very ancient and modern.

Our members taught me so much. They are poor and struggle for money and employment. But they would greet us with big smiles and welcome us into their homes. They are truly wonderful examples to me of courage and faith.

Preaching the Gospel

Our work centered on two areas. One was teaching the gospel to our members and any other Arab Christians that came to our church to learn. We were forbidden to talk about the gospel to any Muslims. The Arab Christians of Jordan are hungry for the truth of the gospel. We had many miracles and the Spirit of the Lord was evident in our work.

One young Arab Christian man, whom we introduced to the teachings of the Church, who was baptized, told me, "When I was baptized I took upon me the name of Jesus Christ. I know that one day I will be in the Lord's presence, and I want Him to be happy with the way I represented Him on the earth." I truly feel that this young man is one of the noble and great ones that we were privileged to find on our mission. Lynn and I agreed that we would have traveled across the earth to find him, and so we did. I believe that we fulfilled a promise that we made to him in the premortal world to find and teach him the gospel. He felt the same way as he learned of the true teachings of the restored Church. He could not learn enough. He will be our friend and brother forever.

In the late evening, Lynn and I would drive to a hill top and look out over the lights of Al Husn and Irbid, Jordan. We would pour out our hearts to Heavenly Father and ask for His guidance. We would say prayers for peace and safety for these precious souls. We could see thousands of lights in front of us and thought of all the people whose lives would shine if they could hear and accept the good news of the gospel of Jesus Christ.

Many times Lynn was asked to give priesthood blessings for the sick. Medical care is limited and for many members not affordable. I was a witness to many instances when the afflicted person was healed immediately. Our members in Jordan have great faith. I miss them.

Humanitarian Work

Our other work, which took much of our time, was humanitarian efforts by the Church to help the non-member poor and needy of Jordan. The senior couple in Amman already received 500 wheelchairs to be given to the Cerebral Palsy Association. We were asked to attend the first ceremony giving them away to the people in Amman. Many parents carried their children into the room. Some of them were fully grown and heavy to carry. Each one received a precious gift of a wheel chair. We knew that most of the children had never had the luxury of movement afforded to them now by this precious gift.

Lynn and I met the directors of the Ministry of Social Development in Hartha, Al Husn and Irbid Jordan. These hardworking and caring men opened the doors for us and introduced us to their volunteer societies who worked with the handicapped. We worked closely with these volunteer societies and requested needed wheelchairs, clothing and other items that our Church supplies free. There are many poor people in Jordan, and these items are greatly needed and appreciated.

We worked with the YWCA in Al Husn, Jordan. We met marvelous and dedicated Christian women and ordered wheelchairs and a container of clothing, quilts, blankets, and medical supplies for distribution by this society. We were delighted to see this Christian organization working in a Muslim country.

Within six months, the three senior couples working in Jordan had requested a total of 1250 wheelchairs with another 1000 coming. In addition, four containers of clothing, blankets, handmade quilts, toys, and medical supplies were requested. Eight hundred fifty kerosene heaters were given away to heat very cold apartments, tents, and caves where the poor and needy lived.

We also started teaching a career workshop for the unemployed and had the materials translated into Arabic. We know that this training helped many of our members obtain better employment and plan for future education leading to better jobs. We learned about local micro-finance programs in Jordan geared to help women and men start their own small businesses. We told our members about these loans and taught them about starting a small business.

LOVING THE PEOPLE, THE LORD, AND EACH OTHER

I learned what it really means to be compassionate and to set aside my own needs and put others first. *"When you are in the service of your fellow beings ye are only in the service of your God"* (Mosiah 2:17). This service was always rewarded with a closeness to my husband Lynn and our Father in Heaven. We were blessed as we worked together. In fact we did everything together. Our hearts were in perfect unity as we served as missionaries. The Lord's promises of joy, light and new understanding were fulfilled in us.

I lost all my fear and reached out in love to those precious people of Jordan, both Christian and Muslim. Truly, Jordan is a wonderful place filled with caring families, marvelous Bible sites to visit plus great bargain shopping in the local suqs. Lynn is great at bargaining for the items we purchased. He always asked for a senior discount.

FAMILY HISTORY FOR OUR JORDANIAN MEMBERS AND MIRACLES OF THE SPIRIT FROM THE OTHER SIDE OF THE VEIL

We also worked with our members on family history. We saw many miracles occur as we did this work with them. We invited one of our member families to come to our apartment to record their family tree. When I typed the name of one of our member's deceased father, I could feel the power of the spirit. I mean the spirit was really powerful. I looked at our member and said to him, "Do you feel the spirit?" He had tears in his eyes and said, "Do YOU feel the spirit?" Then he said, "It is my deceased father. He is here, and he tapped me on my shoulder three times."

He continued, "Sister Nancy, I have been a member of this Church for many years, but it is not until this moment that I understand the truth of the gospel of Jesus Christ about eternal families." He told Lynn and me later that he dreamt of his deceased grandfather three times during the following week. His grandfather asked him, "Why aren't you paying a full tithing?" When he came yet again in a dream and asked the same question, our member said, "Grandfather, you cannot read or write. How do you know I am not paying a full tithing?" The deceased grandfather then said again, "Why aren't you paying a full tithing!" So he promised to pay a full tithing if his deceased grandfather would leave him alone.

Almost all of our members had dreams of their ancestors. The gathering of their names turned the hearts of the children to the fathers in a labor of love.

BIBLE SITES IN JORDAN

We visited over forty Bible sites in Jordan. Many of them were in remote parts of the country where Jewish prophets lived and worked, and Jesus Christ performed miracles.

- We were at the Jordan River where Jesus was baptized by John the Baptist.
- We visited the place where John the Baptist was beheaded.
- Where Elijah the prophet was born and raised.
- Abbila, a Decapolis city, where Jesus healed the deaf mute.
- Umm Quays, where Jesus cast out a legion of evil spirits into 2000 pigs.
- Jerash and Amman (Philadelphia), Decapolis cities, where Jesus came.

- Where Moses stood on Mt. Nebo watching his people walk toward the Jordan River and where he was later translated.
- We saw the Dead Sea and the Red Sea and walked along part of the Lehi trail.
- We saw the ancient City of Petra which was started by Esau, son of Isaac.
- We saw the place of the house of Jacob, father of the twelve tribes and went to the place where he wrestled with an angel and obtained the new name of Israel.
- We will never forget our wonder to stand at Solomon's brass foundry where he cast the twelve oxen, the brazen sea, the two huge brass columns for his temple as well as all the brass temple fittings and vessels.

We felt connected with our past and close to the Lord.

From these experiences my understanding of the scriptures greatly expanded. This in itself was marvelous, inspiring, and sacred to me. I would rejoice with Lynn as we read the stories in the Bible and remembered that they actually took place where we were standing. Our hearts intertwined with faith and a united purpose.

I learned what it was like to preach the gospel and learn the missionary discussions. I learned again and again the power of the Spirit to teach when my words failed me. I understood much more clearly that the gospel of Jesus Christ is for everyone and that the truths of God will go forth in the due time of the Lord. I felt the presence of the Spirit when we gave away wheelchairs and the love of God touched their hearts. I learned about another culture and their trials. I learned to be humble, compassionate, and patient.

A SPECIAL YEARNING FOR JERUSALEM

I will always remember the times we stood along the banks of the Dead Sea, in Jordan, looking at the lights of Jerusalem in the distance to the west. Our hearts were touched. I could feel the personal pull toward Jerusalem and the yearning to be there. I thought of the history of the Jewish nation that I was able to visit firsthand during our time in Jordan. I felt a tremendous connection to Jacob, Moses, Elijah, John the Baptist and Jesus Christ. I knew that there was no break in the history or religion of the Jewish people and the gospel of Jesus Christ. My continued studies of the scriptures, my connection to God during these missions, and my spiritual learning combined in this moment to allow me to understand that the knowledge of the Lord was spreading out to all nations. The link between the two worlds, Jewish and Christian, had become one.

CHAPTER 10

Greece Athens Mission, Part Two, Assignment in Athens
(2005)

> And whoso receiveth you, there I will be also, for I will go before your face. I will be on your right hand and on your left, and my Spirit shall be in your hearts, and mine angels round about you, to bear you up. [D&C 84:88]

DIRECTORS OF THE FAMILY HISTORY CENTER IN ATHENS, GREECE

After ten months of working in Jordan, our mission president reassigned us to Athens, Greece to be the directors of the Family History Center. We had already received feelings or premonitions that we would be leaving Jordan and thus were not surprised when he called us.

Another couple was coming to take our place in Jordan, but our hearts were so entwined with the people it was so hard to leave them. I had changed from a scared woman to one whose heart reached out to others without concern for myself. I had learned so much from the members and people of Jordan. I will never forget them.

I also learned how compassionate the Lord is toward His children. I could feel His presence as Lynn and I worked together to further His kingdom. The Spirit converts people, we are only servants that have the privilege of being there and watching the miracles occur.

On February 3, 2005, Lynn and I flew away from Jordan to Athens, Greece. What a change of culture and missionary duties. We were now in a predominantly Greek Orthodox Christian nation.

We arrived in Athens, Greece and found a suitable apartment. We were only going to be there eight months. For the first time, we did not have a car. We were grateful that we did not have to drive in the traffic in Athens. The biggest fear that we had there was that we would get run over by one of thousands of motorcycles that run rampant on the streets. The second problem we had there was walking on the narrow sidewalks that were obstructed with water meters, trees, parked motorcycles, and were usually for one pedestrian only at best. So we walked single file looking down, and we got a lot of exercise.

The public transportation system there was excellent, and we traveled on buses and the metro. We had many interesting experiences. Everyone stared at our missionary badges that were in Greek. Occasionally they would cross themselves when they saw us, and on two occasions people actually jumped up from their bus seats and moved away from us. But most of the time they were just curious. We just smiled and asked if they could speak English which was rare.

Next, how were we to do this family history job? The missionary that had worked in the FHC before us finished his mission and was leaving the next day. He gave us a very quick overview of the computer programs, forms, and equipment. He handed us the keys and left us on our own.

By this time, we already understood that the Lord would help us step-by-step. It took awhile to get organized. In addition to keeping the FHC open two nights a week, we visited the members, took our laptop computer with us, and showed them how to enter their names in the computer database called PAF 5.2 (Personal Ancestral File).

We explained about eternal families and the temple ordinances. Many of our members told us about the dreams they had of their ancestors and their desire to go to the temple on their behalf. We were witnesses to a miracle when Mabinty, the elderly mother of Gordon, one of our members from Sierra Leone, could remember only a few names then remembered six generations of ancestors' names after we said a prayer. How we rejoiced every time she whispered a new name. We know that she felt the Spirit that night. This precious woman was baptized a few months later. Mabinty is now back in Sierra Leone preaching the gospel to her children and grandchildren. Gordon's family, three other families, and a single man went to the Frankfurt Temple a few months later. They did the temple work for 74 of their deceased ancestors and all family members, both dead and alive, were sealed before returning to Athens.

THE CONTINUING MIRACLES OF FAMILY HISTORY WORK

We felt that our family history building was like the entrance to the temple and therefore sacred. It was a place where our members drew closer to their deceased ancestors as they remembered their names and got them ready for their temple ordinances.

We were experiencing miracles as we worked in the field of genealogy. What a great blessing this work is to us and all past and future generations. Those people who work in this field, whether they are members of the Church or not, come to understand the consuming passion that prompts us to find more and more family names and connect them together. This need to remember and honor our ancestors comes because they are not dead but live on as spirits, in the spirit world. It is only their bodies that die. They want to be remembered and be part of an eternal family linked together by holy ordinances only performed in our temples. To our deceased ancestors, this means that they can progress spiritually, repent of their sins, and qualify for a glorious resurrection.

Our lives are not limited to this earth. We live on and learn more and more as we continue our journey. We are ancient spirits inside of our mortal bodies and some day our pre-earth knowledge will be opened again to us, and we will have a full understanding.

I know that Lynn and I have future missions, both on the earth and after we leave here. I rejoice in this knowledge that I have been given. I am grateful that I have an eternal marriage and that our work together will continue on and on. What greater joy can there be than to do this?

BAPTISMS

Counting our work in Jordan and in Greece we list twenty-four baptisms we participated in. Sometimes we found these people, often we taught the lessons or helped in other ways. Some of these people were the great and noble ones who we think excelled in pre-earth life. We gave testimonies to each: "If thou wilt do good, yea, and hold out faithful to the end, thou shalt be saved in the kingdom of God, which is the greatest of all the gifts of God; for there is no gift greater than the gift of salvation" (see D&C 6:13).

THE END OF OUR THIRD MISSION

We were released from this mission on October 4, 2005. The outcome of this mission was marvelous and eternal in its scope. But the most important aspect of this mission was the closeness that Lynn and I had for each other. Our love for each other increased. Our working together as a unit with each other and the Lord became a living reality. We depended on the Lord and He helped us. We grew as a couple in ways that could not have been possible without this mission. I cannot imagine my life without my husband Lynn and rejoice that we will be together for time and all eternity. Knowing this as a certainty is of great comfort to me. We became one with each other and the Lord. This was done through our love for each other, for the Lord and His children in these far away countries.

Our Trip to Israel

We visited Jerusalem, Israel for two weeks on the way home to Salt Lake City, Utah. Visiting Jerusalem was a wonderful and fulfilling experience. I will never forget the lingering picture in my mind of the thousands of Jewish people at the Wailing Wall on Sabbath eve. I remember waiting at the top of the stairway to go down to the area next to the Wailing Wall. We were stopped until the army could make sure the way was safe. I said to a woman next to me, "Thank goodness for a good army." She said, in reply, "Thank goodness for a good God."

We decided to say a prayer for Judah on the Mt. of Olives. We felt impressed to walk into the vast cemetery that overlooks the Old City and the Dome of the Rock. As we entered the cemetery we noticed a sign that said "the burial place of Malachi." How appropriate to have his burial place close to the place of our prayers. We remembered Malachi's words at the end of the Old Testament, "Behold, I will send you Elijah the prophet before the coming of the great and dreadful day of the Lord: And he shall turn the heart of the fathers to the children, and the heart of the children to their fathers, lest I come and smite the earth with a curse" (Malachi 4:5–6).

As we continued to walk into the cemetery, I could feel a very special spirit as we looked out upon thousands of Jewish grave markers. I pictured in my mind the spirits of all these deceased souls turning their hearts to their living descendants wanting their names to be included in their family trees, never to be forgotten.

We selected a place in the cemetery and started to say our prayers. Just as we began our prayer, a family of Orthodox men walked to a spot close to our location and recited the Kaddish for their dead. At the same time, we also could hear the call to prayer from the Muslim minarets. So we were all praying to God, in our own way, at the same time. We were thrilled to consider this type of unexpected unity.

Our time in Jerusalem was precious. We met and had dinner with a marvelous and dedicated Orthodox family. We visited both the ancient Jewish and Christian sites. We walked the streets of the Old City during Yom Kippur and attended services in an Orthodox synagogue. We were grateful for our time there. It is truly a place of spiritual history.

CHAPTER 11

Growing Spiritually

Oh that my words were now written! Oh that they were printed in a book! That they were graven with an iron pen and lead in the rock for ever! I know that my redeemer liveth, and that he shall stand at the latter day upon the earth: And though after my skin worms destroy this body, yet in my flesh shall I see God: Whom I shall see for myself, and mine eyes shall behold, and not another; though my reins be consumed within me. [Job 19:23–27]

WHAT I LEARNED SINCE RAINBOW BRIDGE

I have learned so much since that afternoon at Rainbow Bridge. I know that I am on a spiritual journey as I walk the paths of mortal life. I will have trials, but I now face them with the knowledge of God and His Son, Jesus Christ, to assist me.

Moses saw God in the burning bush. Paul saw the Lord on the road to Damascus. Alma the younger saw the angel of God as described in the Book of Mormon. Joseph Smith saw our Heavenly Father and His Son Jesus Christ and through the Restoration we can see the path back to our heavenly home.

From these momentous events, the course of the lives of these prophets were changed as they served their God. Their resulting testimony of the gospel of Jesus Christ never wavered as shown in the scriptures.

My burning bush experience is just as powerful to me. I did not see God nor His Son Jesus Christ, but I felt Them. I testify that I was given a gift of knowledge at Rainbow Bridge through the Holy Ghost. This knowledge has grown and matured with a true understanding of the nature and purpose of God and Christ through the Restoration of His Church in this modern time.

The Church of Jesus Christ of Latter-day Saints is the only true Church on the face of the whole earth. It has what the Lord intended ancient Judaism to have. Many of the ancient promises have now been fulfilled. I know that the ancient priesthood of God has been restored to righteous men on the earth in our days. The Church has temples, a prophet, and many miracles that occur.

I will quote from my patriarchal blessing. *"Many do not yet know of the true nature of their Messiah, the fact that He has come and that He truly is the Savior of the world. One day they shall know."* I know that the Messiah has come and will return again to the earth. His name is Jesus Christ. He is the Son of God. I know that His name has been falsely used to persecute the Jewish people. His true doctrine is one of love not hate. I know that if we follow the true gospel of Jesus Christ that we will live together in peace and harmony.

FULFILLMENT OF PROMISES FOR THE JEWISH PEOPLE

So who is Jesus Christ? What is the meaning of Judaism? How are they related? What is the plan of salvation?

When I was a young Jewish girl, I wanted to fully understand Judaism. What I learned gave me only a small glimpse of the beauty and purpose of God's ancient religion. We studied the knowledge of God that was revealed through our ancient prophets like Moses. But my most sacred yearnings went unanswered. Learning and studying these ancient scriptures did not answer my most basic questions that I had in my heart. Where was the power of God now? Where is His glory? Who is God? What does it mean to be Jewish? What is our future?

Did I abandon my religion when I joined The Church of Jesus Christ of Latter-day Saints? *I say to you no.* I now have a fuller understanding of God's plan built upon the foundation of my original Jewish faith. I now understand how He tried to guide us, to give us the priesthood and all of His knowledge; but we, as a people, rejected it. He tried again and again, over the centuries, through His prophets, but we listened only occasionally. Now our religion has become an empty shell filled with traditions instead of spiritual power—and rote ceremonies, devoid of the Holy Spirit, in the place of our ancient living faith. This is all that we have left. For the most part the Jewish people have remained faithful to their Jewish religion through centuries of persecution. However, Jews also have the promise of a glorious restoration in the latter days.

We Jewish people used to have a temple. We had miracles from God. We had the Aaronic Priesthood given by God's authority to Aaron and passed down through his bloodline. We had prophets, but where are they now? We substituted a rabbi and synagogue in the place of priesthood authority and temples.

The Jewish people suffered and died to bring the world both the Old and New Testaments. Through their lineage came our Savior Jesus Christ and many of the apostles. It was the Jews, the ancient covenant people of the Lord, who brought these scriptures and knowledge to the world. But what thanks have they been given by the Christian community? (2 Nephi 29:3–10)

I now understand that God has a Son, just as our prophets told us, and why the sacrifice of Jesus Christ was necessary. With the additional knowledge that I have been given through the teachings of The Church of Jesus Christ of Latter-day Saints and both ancient and modern prophets, I understand God's eternal plan for the Jewish people.

If they choose, they can have the strength and power of the ancient or higher priesthood; not just a few chosen priests like Aaron or Levi, but all worthy men to receive the higher priesthood of Melchizedek.

The complete designs of God are not known to me, but I can tell you without any hesitation that God lives and He has a perfect plan for us and our world. Prayer and communication with God is active, on-going, and needed. The temple in all its spiritual glory has been restored. The priesthood authority from God is once again on the earth. We have a living prophet to lead and guide us. Israel is being gathered as foretold. Miracles happen, and God's covenant with us and all humanity is being fulfilled through The Church of Jesus Christ of Latter-day Saints.

My Testimony

There comes a time in our lives when we need God. We need something more to define our lives and give us purpose. We are mortal and live upon the plane of this earth seeking wisdom and knowledge.

How much richer our lives can become if we extend our knowledge beyond this world and take the leap of faith forward into the kingdom of God. How much greater is our hope in our future if we know that we are children of God. Why only strive for the things of the world when there is a much greater hope that will come to us through our Savior Jesus Christ.

We have been called upon to repent and be baptized. We have received instruction through modern prophets who now have the authority and power of God, on the earth, to perform a valid baptism and give us the gift of the Holy Ghost that will last beyond death. From this first step we can start along the path back to our Father in Heaven and his celestial kingdom. My patriarchal blessing says, "You may now walk in the light of the Savior, as you now begin that special journey that will lead you back to the presence of your God."

Over and over, our Father in Heaven has tried to communicate with us, but we neglect to respond. We have forgotten that we can communicate with Him and have replaced this with rote prayers.

We have received commandments to depend not on just our mortal flesh but on our spiritual natures. We are told that we must choose good from evil, and if we choose good our lives will be filled with happiness and joy. When we choose evil and sin we wonder why our lives are a mess. Hearken to the words of the Lord and bless yourselves and your family by rejecting sin and evil, and embrace the fullness of the gospel. Keep the commandments of the Lord, then you will rejoice and be happy.

It is not rocket science to understand that we are immortal spirits inside of our bodies. That we lived before the creation of this world as spirit children of our Heavenly Father. We lived before, and we will continue to live after our mortal lives end.

This is the time of testing to see if we are worthy to return home to our Father's house, for no unclean thing can dwell there. Why would we choose only the temporary riches of the earth when we can obtain the permanent riches of exaltation and eternal life? Why would we limit ourselves to things that corrupt us and ignore the things of repentance, salvation, and a glorious life to come. Real success, in this life, is a family and children filled with love one for another who live gospel principles and are sealed together for all eternity.

But in the end, I believe that God's ancient covenant people (Jewish people) will someday know Him. Their minds will open like a flower that blossoms and continues to bloom. The paths of their minds will be unlocked, and pure knowledge will flow into them and remind them of their true God. They will all have a burning bush experience like mine. They will hear His voice and feel His presence through the Holy Ghost and awaken to the knowledge of the Lord Jesus Christ, the Son of God. Here are His words of invitation,

> And again, the Lord shall utter his voice out of heaven, saying: Hearken, O ye nations of the earth, and hear the words of that God who made you.
>
> O, ye nations of the earth, how often would I have gathered you together as a hen gathereth her chickens under her wings, but ye would not!

> How oft have I called upon you by the mouth of my servants, and by the ministering of angels, and by mine own voice, and by the voice of thunderings, and by the voice of lightnings, and by the voice of tempests, and by the voice of earthquakes, and great hailstorms, and by the voice of famines and pestilences of every kind, and by the great sound of a trump, and by the voice of judgment, and by the voice of mercy all the day long, and by the voice of glory and honor and the riches of eternal life, and would have saved you with an everlasting salvation, *but ye would not.* [D&C 43:23–25, emphasis added]

When this day comes, I pray that they will accept of the fullness of the gospel of Jesus Christ. All of it. That they may be crowned with glory, immortality, and eternal lives. That they will be the children of God, repentant, redeemed, and exalted. We live for this glorious day of promise. The power of God will be manifest once again in the ancient land of Israel.

We have the following promises from the holy prophets:

> In that day [the last days] shall the Lord defend the inhabitants of Jerusalem; and he that is feeble among them at that day shall be as David . . . .
>
> I will seek to destroy all the nations that come against Jerusalem.
>
> And I will pour out upon the house of David, and upon the inhabitants of Jerusalem, the spirit of grace and supplications: and they shall look upon me whom they have pierced and they shall mourn for him, as one mourneth for his only son . . . . [Zechariah 12:8–10]

> Then shall the Lord set his foot upon this mount [Mt. of Olives in Jerusalem at the Lord's second coming] and it shall cleave in twain, and the earth shall tremble, and reel to and fro and the heavens also shall shake. . . .
>
> And then shall the Jews look upon me and say: What are these wounds in thine hands and feet?
>
> Then shall they know that I am the Lord; for I will say unto them: These wounds are the wounds with which I was wounded in the house

of my friends. I am he who was lifted up. I am Jesus Christ that was crucified. I am the Son of God.

And then shall they weep...because they persecuted their king....

For the Lord shall be in their midst, and his glory shall be upon them, and he will be their king and their lawgiver. [D&C 45:48, 51–53, 59]

Judah, after their pain, shall be sanctified in holiness before the Lord, to dwell in his presence day and night forever and ever. [D&C 133:35]

Glory to those who stand firm on the foundation of the gospel and finally return home to live with our Father in Heaven and His Son Jesus Christ. Glory be to our Father whose mercy extends into our world and beyond.

I leave you my testimony that what I have written here is true, in the name of Jesus Christ, amen.

No unhallowed hand can stop the work of God from progressing. Persecutions may rage, mobs may combine, armies may assemble, calumny may defame, but the truth of God will go forth boldly, nobly and independent till it has penetrated every continent, visited every clime, swept every country and sounded in every ear, till the purposes of God shall be accomplished and the Great Jehovah shall say the work is done.

—Joseph Smith, the Prophet,
The Wentworth Letter, 1842